What Are They Saying About Scripture and Ethics?

(Fully Revised and Expanded Edition)

William C. Spohn

PAULIST PRESS
New York and Mahwah, N.J.

Cover design by Tim McKeen

Library of Congress Cataloging-in-Publication Data

Spohn, William C.
    What are they saying about Scripture and ethics? / by William C. Spohn. —Fully rev. and expanded ed.
        p.   cm.
    Includes bibliographical references.
    ISBN 0-8091-3609-0 (alk. paper)
    1. Christian ethics—History—20th century. 2. Ethics in the Bible. 3. Christian ethics—Biblical teaching. 4. Bible—Criticism, interpretation, etc.—History—20th century. I. Title.
BJ1231.S64 1995   95-22768
241.5.dc20   CIP

Published by Paulist Press
997 Macarthur Boulevard
Mahwah, NJ 07430

Printed and bound in the
United States of America

Contents

Foreword to the Second Edition

This second edition comes ten years after the first and includes the significant developments in the area of Scripture and ethics which have occurred since 1984. It incorporates most of the major figures treated in the earlier edition insofar as they continue to influence the contemporary discussion. Since most of these authors have continued to write on this topic, I have substantially rewritten the majority of the book and added new theologians whose works have appeared recently. The only exception to this approach is the chapter on "The Command of God" whose major figures, Karl Barth and Dietrich Bonhoeffer, continue to influence certain segments of the Christian community. The first edition contained a chapter that centered on the work of H. Richard Niebuhr; this edition has integrated some of that material into other chapters whose major figures develop the groundbreaking insights of Niebuhr. The new introductory chapter focuses on the problem of hermeneutics which has become central to the use of Scripture and proposes an analytical framework that structures the rest of the book. It asks: *What* material is selected from Scripture, *why* is it interpreted in this fashion, and *how* is it applied to contemporary life? The final chapter of this second edition, entitled "Scripture as Basis for Responding Love," centers on the question of how Jesus of Nazareth, as portrayed in Scripture, can be normative for Christian life. Although it retains the title of the original chapter, its contents represent my current reflections on a constructive approach to the use of Scripture in ethics.

When theologians turn to Scripture for moral guidance they are not acting like moral philosophers. They do not begin with a theory of ethics but with a canonical text which is authoritative because it is inspired by

1

God. Christians turn to Scripture to discover more than the right thing to do; they want to act in a way that responds to the One who has entered their lives. Systems of ethics begin with a fundamental principle or value. The Gospel begins with a person who claims that he himself is the "norm" we are to follow when he calls: "Come, follow me."

In both the Old Testament and the New a new way of life is presented to God's people to follow which is inseparable from the history that has revealed God. (The texts which are "the Hebrew Scriptures" for Jews are "the Old Testament" for Christians. Since I am writing as a Christian theologian, I will refer to the "Old Testament" not to impose an alien designation on those texts, but to remind the reader that the Hebrew Scriptures are also Scripture for Christians.) The use of Scripture in Christian ethics, therefore, must be rooted in that history and the One it reveals. The theologian faces a host of questions that need not bother the philosopher: What texts are central to this way of life? How are they to be interpreted in light of what we know about God and Christ? What are the morally revealing dimensions of biblical literature (symbols, narratives, parables, poems, and the like), and how do they color our reading of the rules and principles in Scripture? What is the appropriate community context in which to discover and live out this way of life? No wonder that theologians have a lot to say about using Scripture in ethics. Even less surprising is the lack of agreement among them.

In the chapters that follow we will examine five typical ways that Christian theologians are employing Scripture in ethics. I hope that this will lead the reader to discover some of the richness that biblical studies have made available to Christian ethics. The field of Christian ethics in the latter part of the twentieth century has begun to assimilate the advances made in biblical scholarship in the past century. Even more importantly, most of the new methods of biblical scholarship recognize that the Bible requires faithful engagement as well as historical criticism. This is a particularly fruitful time for Christian ethics and should lead to a richer appreciation of Scripture for all believers. Every form of biblical literature, from love poetry to parable, evokes a response to God and to others. The text does not lead us into a faithful way of life; that is the accomplishment of God's grace. But the text can alter our vision and our feelings, our characteristic ways of evaluating and acting, so that we respond more fully to the One the Bible reveals.

I am grateful to the theologians who have enhanced my reading of God's Word; to my students who challenge me to understand it anew; to my friends and colleagues at the Jesuit School of Theology at Berkeley and Santa Clara University who call me to be faithful, in particular Martha Ellen Stortz and Tom Leininger who have greatly aided this second edition. Special gratitude goes to the Jesuit community at Santa Clara University and the Louis Bannan S.J. Foundation whose generous hospitality during 1982–83 made the first edition of this work possible. A similar thanks to the university's administration who made the second edition possible by appointing its author John Nobili, S.J., University Professor in 1992.

Introduction

This book will examine how theologians use Scripture in writing about ethics. We will study the use of Scripture in ethics, a different task from studying the ethics in Scripture. For the latter we would turn to exegetical works like Wolfgang Schrage's *The Ethics of the New Testament*, or Willi Marxsen's *New Testament Foundations for Christian Ethics*.[1] The theologians we will examine build on the exegetical studies of their day. Instead of asking, for example, what Paul meant in Romans 13:1–7, they will raise the question about what bearing it should have on Christians today. It will be helpful to distinguish theology from the life of faith and ethics from morality. The lived experience of faith and morality are the foundation of the more abstract and systematic discussions of theology and ethics. Since they are meant to enrich the experience of faith and moral life, putting theological and ethical theories into practice is their final test.

What does Scripture have to say to us today? In the final decades of the twentieth century the focus of biblical studies has changed from what the text meant originally to what it means for readers today. The historical critical method which held sway for most of the century tried to establish what the biblical writings meant to their original audiences. Some scholars adopted a religiously neutral stance to emulate the objective methods of the physical sciences. They refused to draw any theological or moral conclusions from their historical research. Since their form of history was descriptive rather than normative, it could not answer the religious and moral questions which believers bring to Scripture.

More recently, biblical scholars have moved away from relying exclusively on historical criticism, pointing out that contemporary science has forsaken the ideal of objective neutrality as an impossible standard. The biblical texts are not inert records to be analyzed by detached observers, but classic texts of a living culture that each generation dialogues with. Just like nature, the Bible answers the questions which humans pose, questions which are inevitably laden with presuppositions and shaped by particular interests. Those presuppositions may be positive resources for appreciating the text. Jews and Christians do not approach the Bible primarily as a library of ancient texts, but as "Scripture," namely the authoritative document of their tradition which mediates the self-communication of God. Someone who is open to being transformed by the Other who may be encountered through the biblical text will enter the dialogue with the Bible with a very different attitude than someone who approaches its texts with religious indifference or skepticism. For the first person the Bible will be "Scripture," where the skeptic will treat it as merely an historical artifact.[2]

There are many forms of literature in the Bible besides history: poetry, prophetic rhetoric, apocalyptic, parable, wisdom, legal codes, exemplary fiction, doctrinal instruction, etc. In fact, history in the modern sense is not the primary intention of the texts. The growing appreciation of this diversity led to a number of new forms of literary criticism that study the dynamics of the texts: contextual criticism, rhetorical and narrative studies, sociological and psychological approaches. Where exegesis studies the formation of the text, these newer methods begin from the final form of the text and investigate its impact on the readers.

Nevertheless, the conversation should begin with the best results of historical method in presenting the original meaning of the texts. The meaning of a specific scriptural passage *then* has a controlling influence on its meaning *now*. "It is a general rule of proper textual interpretation that a text should be read for what its author meant to say and what its first readers or hearers would have heard it say," writes Mennonite theologian John Howard Yoder. Roman Catholic biblical scholarship also has affirmed the primacy of the original meaning.[3] Sound exegesis of the original meaning is the initial defense against "eisegesis" which twists the text to say whatever the reader wishes. The biblical authors and communities wrestled with the moral issues of their particular times and places. If today's readers ignore these contexts, they will have no precedent for addressing the particular questions of their own society. As we shall see there are four principal elements in using Scripture in ethics. At one pole stands a) the faith community that produced the text and b) the world represented in the text (the social, economic, political forms of the time); at the other pole stands c) the contemporary faith community and d) its own "world."

Present day believers cannot merely copy the original solutions. In order to be both free and faithful, they reason by analogy from the earlier interaction which is witnessed in the biblical text to a similar response to the challenges of their own times. As we shall see in the final chapter, analogical thinking relies on imagination and the ability to discern similarities and differences between one situation and another.

The author's intentions should not restrict subsequent interpretations because later generations will ask questions of the Bible or other classic texts that the author could not have foreseen. Since genuine classics address common human experience with literary richness, they always have a "surplus of meaning" which makes them fertile sources of new insights. Classical stories and symbols resonate far beyond the particular time and place in which they were composed and even beyond the explicit consciousness of their authors.[4]

Later interpretations may well bring out meanings that were latent in the text. For example, our contemporary appreciation of human equality overrides Paul's cautious advice to slaves. We take his sweeping affirmation that in Christ there is no longer Jew or Greek, slave or free, male or female (Gal 3:28) as a more fundamental moral principle than the Letter to the Ephesians' advice that slaves should obey their masters with the same sincerity that they would give to Christ (Eph 6:5). Because equality in Christ is more central to Pauline theology it should be taken more seriously than time-bound advice about maintaining an ancient domestic order which kept women and slaves in subordination. The trajectory of Paul's teaching of equality is already set by the biblical text, even if it would take centuries before the Christian community would see that slavery and the subordination of women were incompatible with human dignity. Those who are confident that the Spirit of Christ guided the community's tradition can appeal to subsequent developments in order to correct the limitations in Paul's writings. Since the same Spirit that inspired the authors of Scripture still inspires the use of Scripture in the Church today, believers can hope to maintain faithful continuity with those early believers and also to develop beyond them where it is necessary.

The Hermeneutical Challenge

How should we move from these texts composed in ancient cultures to address the moral questions of our time and place? While historical critical studies can strive to determine what the biblical text meant, they cannot tell us what it should mean for us. Literary and social criticism can unpack "the world of the text" but they fall short of spelling out its contemporary meaning. In order to discover what transforming truth and promise Scripture has for us we turn to *hermeneutics*, that is, engaged interpretation of authoritative texts. The line between using Scripture in ethics and examining the ethics in Scripture has become blurred by the emerging discipline of hermeneutics, which goes beyond exegesis to the interaction between today's reader and the biblical text. It is used here to signify the critical interaction of readers and the text, and how its truth "comes home" to them.[5] Like any great literature, the Bible requires critical study to unpack its richness, yet it should lead to religious engagement because of Scripture's unique character. It is the Word of God in human words. Its authorship is not merely human, and it discloses not simply truth about life, but the One who is the source of life and truth.

The first moral challenge of hermeneutics is to acknowledge the presuppositions and specific interests that inevitably shape our reading of Scripture. The concerns we bring to the text are lenses that highlight certain dimensions and obscure others. Hermeneutics warns us of the danger of projecting our own concerns onto the text so that it only echoes our unexamined presuppositions. This perennial temptation affects every reader, from those engaged in theology that advocates for the oppressed to those who bracket social concerns and yet benefit from the status quo of unjust structures. Since "there is no innocent eye," we cannot achieve a neutral or exhaustive reading of the biblical text or any other work.

Every inquiry moves to some extent around the "hermeneutical circle"; that is, the data answers the questions we ask and gets massaged into the procedures that we employ. Self-critical awareness of our own perspective (confessional commitments, social location, class, gender, race, nationality, etc.) can prevent this "hermeneutical circle" from becoming a vicious one. On the one hand, if the reader merely seeks to find biblical support for moral positions arrived at on other grounds, Scripture no longer functions as an authoritative source. It becomes not a challenge but an echo. On the other, our initial presuppositions are not always suspect. Often the concerns that prompt us to turn to Scripture, like commitment to liberating the oppressed or a desire for a deeper relationship with God, arise from a biblically informed perspective. Even in these cases, Scripture should always be a two-edged sword that can challenge the reader's presuppositions. The encounter between the reader and the way of life embodied in the text is not always smooth; sometimes it is more a collision than a fusion.

Thomas W. Ogletree points out that contemporary readers bring several "preunderstandings" about what constitutes morality to the biblical text. Whether we are conscious of it or not, our culture accepts three approaches to morality: deontology, which stresses the rational application of universal rules; perfectionism, which attends to the role of virtues and vices in personal identity and development; and consequentialism, which looks to results to justify an action or policy.[6] Although the most common form of moral discourse in America is consequentialism, Ogletree finds this focus on results absent from biblical texts. Consequently, if we read Scripture with a commonsense utilitarian preunderstanding of morality, we will miss most of what it has to offer.

Ogletree describes three stages of reflection on biblical texts for moral insight which make up the process of hermeneutics:

1. *Recognizing our point of view:* "an explicit account of salient preunderstandings of the moral life" that brings to light our way of looking at the world. (Writers in hermeneutics often stress that raising this "horizon" to conscious awareness means acknowledging biases that stem from race, class, gender, and the like.)

2. *Recognizing biblical points of view:* "a reconstruction of pivotal themes of biblical faith, ordered with reference to those preunderstandings" which includes careful study of the socio-historical contexts of pertinent biblical texts, and

3. *Bringing the two together:* "constructive suggestions toward a 'fusion' in contemporary life and thought of these two worlds of meaning."[7]

This final step is often called a "fusion of horizons" between that of the text and that of the reader. The dialogue with the text does not lead to a simple transfer from one worldview or horizon to another, but to discovering shared meanings and critical disagreements in a creative interpretation which expands the world of meaning of the reader. It opens him or her to the transforming action of God in relation to the particular issues of the present; these issues in turn bring out new meaning in the text.

Unfortunately, many works on biblical hermeneutics recommend the "fusion of horizons" without describing how to do it. They bring us to the edge of ethics and then pull back since they concentrate more on the virtues and vices of handling the texts rather than on the means to carry the message into action that will transform us and the world. The hermeneutical conversation is inescapably moral as J.I.H. McDonald writes, "texts raise moral issues; ethics considers the treatment of such issues, in ancient and modern settings; interpreters consider the moral consequences of their interpretations."[8] For feminist critic Sandra M. Schneiders, the goal of hermeneutical reflection is not primarily to grasp the world *of* the text or the world *behind* the text, namely the horizon of the authors. It seeks engagement with the world *before* the text, that is, the life it introduces us into. Hermeneutics aims at "appropriation…an experience of conversion by participation in the world before the text."[9] Every great work of literature or theater invites us into an alternative reality where new possibilities are disclosed for our lives. The New Testament presents a different way of living, which it calls in various places "life in Christ," "discipleship," "living the Truth," and "the reign of God." Since appropriation means making my own what is genuinely "other," I first need some critical distance from the text to know that its world is not my world. The biblical "text must maintain its identity, its 'strangeness,' which both gifts and challenges the reader. It must be allowed to say what it says, regardless of whether this is comfortable or assimilable by the reader."[10]

Critical distance is as necessary to appreciate Paul as it is to appreciate Hamlet. If, however, I keep my distance in critical consciousness, it would be like studying Shakespeare's text but never enjoying a performance of it. The truth of Hamlet would not come home to me in a transforming way because my imagination, emotions, and personal identity would not be engaged. Once informed by critical study, I need to move beyond it to what Paul Ricouer called "the second naiveté," where I can appreciate that the new world disclosed in the encounter can transform my life. Probably all Christians have been affected by Scripture in this deep way at some time, otherwise they would not believe that it is the Word of God. Effective worship services and profound prayer can convey the truth of Scripture immediately and transparently, as Schneiders describes:

> The parable is my story, redescribing my world as challenged and transformed by the values of the reign of God. The psalm is my song, the words lent to my soul and my tongue as I exult in the goodness and beauty of God and creation or cry out in agony before the injustice of life. The prophecy is spoken to our historical reality, judging injustice and promising salvation to me and the community in which I live.[11]

How do we accept this invitation to an alternative reality which is glimpsed at such moments? How does profound aesthetic appreciation lead to constructive action? As hermeneutics moves into ethics, quite different answers are offered. Whether we appropriate the new vision by the route of personal integration or whether social action takes precedence will be determined by the theological and moral commitments of our particular theology. Different responses can be expected from the rich variety of biblical resources, but to spell them out, we need to go beyond hermeneutics to theological ethics.

The Community Interprets Scripture

When we recognize that the biblical texts are addressed to communities, we cannot approach them as isolated individuals. Unfortunately, a good deal of hermeneutical writings presume that an individual reader is approaching a printed work of literature. The rhetorical setting of most of Scripture is quite different: they were proclaimed to communities and were produced by communities over an extended period of oral communication and editing. Recent studies of the social setting of the New Testament insist on a *contextual reading*: more careful attention must be paid to the economy and social character of the various communities that produced the canonical traditions. Only then will we be able to move from their context to our own. Lisa Sowle Cahill describes the "hermeneutics of social embodiment" favored by Wayne E. Meeks: "it investigates the patterns of interaction between biblical narratives and their generating environment, then seeks appropriate recapitulations of such patterns in the contemporary church."[12] Meeks is spelling out the fourfold process described above: a) the original community confronting b) its world guides c) present day communities reacting with d) their world. Faced with today's moral tensions, a given faith community should investigate how NT communities fashioned a Christian approach to the particular economic and social world they inhabited. In this fourfold conversation of social ethics the locus of moral discernment is always communal. The connection between what the text meant morally in its setting and what it means today must be the community. NT mandates to achieve justice by almsgiving and to practice nonviolence must become enacted in "coherent social embodiments of a community formed by Scripture."[13]

We shall see in the final chapter that the analogical imagination moves from one situation to another by discerning patterns or paradigms in the first instance and then seeking a similar pattern in the novel setting. Today's communities move by analogy from the responses of the apostolic communities to new and faithful practices that respond to the social institutions of this world. How do they know which biblical patterns to follow? They must choose which ones to emulate according to normative reflection based upon the other sources of moral theology, namely tradition, philosophical ethics, and pertinent empirical data. *Tradition* represents the accumulated wisdom of the community in living the gospel. It includes major theologians, saints and prophetic voices along with official Church teaching. Philosophical *ethics* incorporates the best rational accounts of human value and obligation; biblically inspired actions must not violate these basic human standards. *Empirical data* from the social, biological, and personality sciences provide the descriptive foundation for normative reflection guided by Scripture, tradition, and ethics. Accurate factual data needs to ground thought about what we ought to do and become.

From Hermeneutics to Ethics

In the past decade Scripture scholars are starting to use hermeneutics to bridge exegesis and ethics. Freed from the academic restrictions of traditional historical criticism, they have started to spell out what biblical texts can mean to us today. When many Christian ethicists seem intimidated by the complexity of using Scripture in their constructive ethical writings, biblical scholars are drawing conclusions for contemporary moral issues from the interaction of biblical communities and their contexts. Unfortunately, they are often more conscious of their psychological, sociological, and economic presuppositions than their ethical assumptions in making this transfer. While they acknowledge their own "social location," they are unable to specify what their "preunderstandings" about morality are, which Ogletree has shown will profoundly affect their reading of the text. They move from the moral reflection found in Scripture to moral implications for today without passing through *ethics*, that is, the critical study of human value and obligation. Many assume without argument that ethics is about social transformation, others that it is about universal norms, and still others that ethics is about personal transformation and the development of character.

In order to show how hermeneutics works in theological ethics, let me propose a way to analyze ethical arguments that appeal to Scripture. The process of moving from any classic text, including Scripture, to the world of the reader necessarily involves three distinct but related moments. These moments provide a framework for analyzing how a theologian uses Scripture. First, *what* text is selected, or what portions of the text are focused upon? Secondly, *why* have these texts been chosen? The author should acknowledge the theological vision which makes these texts important. Finally, *how* should interaction with these texts make a difference for the reader? We move from biblical text to action by passing through some form of ethics. Are moral principles and rules the appropriate path to action, or should we look for ideals and moral values, or develop virtuous dispositions to translate our engagement with Scripture into practice? Ethics considers these questions more explicitly than hermeneutics does. There are, therefore, three steps in analyzing the use of Scripture in writings on theological ethics:

1. *Selection:* What biblical material does the author include and what is left out? Are some types of literature, authors, or periods considered more authoritative than others? Turning to the Bible for moral guidance is not like reading a single book because it is a library of books composed over thirteen hundred years and several different cultures. We have to make selections and be clear about our reasons for doing so. Since all theologians have their own "canon within the canon," they should provide some rationale for their choices. At the same time, they should be open to testimony from the rest of the canon which might not echo their own preferences. The diversity of the biblical canon balances off themes and emphases within it. Regrettably, this is often overlooked: theologians who favor the radical religious urgency of prophetic literature do not often advert to its relation to the commonsense worldliness of wisdom literature. Selections are made in a variety of areas:

a. Particular *authors* are given greater importance. For example, Martin Luther found the key to Christian moral life in what Paul taught in Romans and Galatians about Law and Gospel. By contrast, liberation theologians sometimes ignore Paul in preference to the prophets and synoptic accounts of Jesus' public ministry. The high Christology and symbolic universe of John's Gospel appeal more to Roman Catholic than Protestant ethicists whose theology has been more influenced by critics who dismissed the Gospel of John because it was not "historical." Walter Brueggemann has criticized the historical books of the OT as apologists for the status quo of the monarchy, while turning to the prophets and Job for the authentic expressions of outrage and grief that open the people to the transforming action of God.[14]

b. Different *eras* within the canon are given greater or lesser authority. For the Anabaptists, the more radical wing of the Reformation, the "New Law of Christ" rendered the Hebrew Scriptures largely obsolete. Some redaction critics consider only the most primitive layers of the synoptic gospels to be authentic. The "Jesus Seminar" of critics has produced an edition of the gospels and the

Gospel of Thomas which uses five different colors of ink to distinguish what Jesus doubtless said from what he might have said from what he could not have said.[15] Many modern scholars consider the post-Pauline epistles as dilutions of gospel freedom under the impetus of ecclesiastical institutionalization.

c. Biblical revelation occurs in distinctive ways through the different *literary genres*, as Paul Ricoeur and other literary critics point out.[16] Prophecy addresses the reader as divine self-disclosure; narrative treats foundational historical events as the paradigms of God's action; legal codes express God's call and requirement for holiness; wisdom literature locates the community ethos in the regular patterns of the *cosmos*; and hymnic discourse articulates and forms emotions that will respond to the divine reality. Apocalyptic, instructional discourse, myth, parable, metaphor, and gospel have been added to the list of literary forms which operate in a distinctive manner.

In the past twenty years, scholars have charted the ways in which each of these forms of discourse shapes moral consciousness. Is metaphor, however, more fundamental for moral vision than prophecy, or is narrative the key to a biblical ethics? The different genres work together to impact the audience of Scripture, as when canticle and psalm celebrate lyrically the narrative of Exodus or Exile. The type of ethics which the theologian prefers, which is usually unacknowledged, will influence which literary genre the author concentrates on.

Passages that explicitly treat a moral problem rarely exhaust the biblical testimony on any given subject. One must also attend to broader moral themes which augment, qualify or correct the specific moral norms on the problem. For example, even though Jesus has little to say in the gospels about sexuality beyond an unqualified opposition to adultery, the larger themes of covenant love, service, God's fidelity to promises, forgiveness, and the redemption of the individual in community help to supplement and give a theological context to NT sexual norms--and may provide the theological foundation to interpret them in new ways as new contexts and empirical understandings arise.

Some authors avoid the problem of selection by attempting to harmonize contradictory moral directives in the canon. In Romans 13:1–7, for example, Paul counsels a patient acceptance of civic duties on the grounds that the state is ordained by God for certain functions. The author of Revelation considers the same Roman state to be demonic and unequivocally condemned by God. While it may be tempting to harmonize the two passages in order to present a unified biblical perspective on civil authority, the differences between them should not be ignored. According to Richard B. Hays, "Romans 13 and Revelation 13 are *not* two complementary expressions of a single New Testament understanding of the state; rather they represent radically different assessments of the relation of the Christian community to the empire."[17] The theologian writing a theology of secular power and responsibility must choose between the two texts or reject them both.

2. *Interpretation:* The what? question yields to the *why?* question. Why should we consider these texts authoritative for morality? The answer comes from the theological themes and methodological commitments which the author has made. Any consistent theology hangs together around particular theological symbols and doctrines. Basic images of God, human experience, and the world, the relation of sin and grace (or grace and nature) provide the warrants for selecting particular biblical materials and using them in a certain way. Prescriptions for moral practice drawn from Scripture depend directly upon the theologian's central doctrinal commitments. Richard N. Longenecker asserts that theological interpretations of Paul's remarks on women which are based on creation differ sharply from interpretations centered on redemption: "Where the former is stressed, subordination and submission are usually emphasized—sometimes even silence; where the latter is stressed, freedom, mutuality, and equality are usually emphasized."[18]

David Kelsey has shown how theological hermeneutics relies on the imagination to establish a consistent point of view which determines how Scripture will be used. The author's philosophical and doctrinal priorities determine which texts are selected for consideration. Because Scripture and tradition offer a rich variety of approaches, basic methodological options must be made in order to construct a consistent theology. Which image of God is central: creator, lawgiver, merciful parent, predestinating sovereign, liberator? Does Christology rest primarily on the incarnation or on the cross and resurrection? Does the grace of Christ restore natural human inclinations to what their Creator intended? Or does grace radically transform them since they are thoroughly corrupted by sin? Is the Christian community primarily a haven for the broken, an intensely committed band of disciples that is an exemplary light to the world, or a servant of human justice and solidarity? Obviously, these are not the only theological alternatives that could be cited.

Ogletree, for instance, candidly acknowledges that his selection of the synoptic gospels and Paul "represents a judgment concerning what is most distinctive and interesting about the Bible so far as contemporary Christian ethics is concerned. In these materials we find the most significant challenges to the conventional wisdom of contemporary society and culture."[19] He orders the diversity of Scripture around certain theological convictions and fundamental understandings about morality and human community. The synoptic gospels and the pre-exilic prophets develop an eschatological vision which stands in moral tension with present realities. Paul breaks from the Israelite tradition of law by stressing the reality of divine promise which turns our moral reflection to the underlying relationship to God and Christ rather than obedience to particular imperatives.[20] Ogletree stands consciously within the Reformation tradition of Law and Gospel, where priority is given to grace over obedience to law. His rearticulation of the traditional dichotomy into "Law and Promise" is also influenced by his ethical method, as we shall see below.

Roman Catholic moralists have begun to incorporate Scripture into moral theology which had been a predominantly philosophical, natural law ethics. They have been more explicit about why they use biblical materials than Protestants who have approached Christian ethics from the principle that it was *sola Scriptura*.

The main difficulty in the current shift of Christian ethics to hermeneutics and biblical commentary is that their practitioners are often not as forthcoming about, or sometimes even aware of, their theological commitments as systematic theologians are expected to be. While the contextual or socio-political approach to biblical hermeneutics and ethics has become widely accepted, it rests on a whole series of theological and ethical options for which reasons should be given.

3. *Application:* The *why?* question in turn yields to the *how?* query. How are these texts, so interpreted, to be applied practically? Some particular form of ethics must provide the conduit from theory to practice: Scripture provides rules and principles, commends certain

values and ideals, engenders certain habits, and exemplifies specific community practices. (Obviously, these are not mutually exclusive moral categories.) What should be the main vehicle for moral application: the graced imagination, prayerful intuition, inferential reason, or calculation of consequences? If all are employed, how do they work together? If the anticipated results violate certain moral principles, for example, which should we follow? These practical problems cannot be resolved by reading the Bible alongside the *New York Times* and intuiting what the moral response should be.

Exegetes and theologians often take a great deal of moral philosophy for granted when it comes to application. Hermeneutics seems content with bringing the reader to a deep aesthetic encounter with the text without helping to determine what to do with what has been appropriated. As Ogletree points out, our culture has a variety of preunderstandings about ethics which remain unexamined by many authors. The different types of moral approaches may be seen as mutually exclusive, although they need not be. A knowledge of moral principles and virtuous habits of character are equally necessary for moral maturity; moral principles expressed as human rights are indispensable for setting the outer limits of social policy, but close attention to consequences will be more useful for framing policy details.

The type of ethics assumed in the application frequently determines the selection. Adhering to a single ethical approach can blind one to the richness of Scripture since it contains examples of each of these approaches. Martin Luther's deep suspicion of legalism minimized the role of law for those who have gospel faith. As a result he reinterpreted the Decalogue and Sermon on the Mount as "disposition ethics," mandates about inner attitudes rather than prohibitions of certain acts. The fifth commandment is not primarily about killing but about meekness and respect for the welfare of others. (In the "Small Catechism" Luther gets more specific about certain actions that are directed toward the neighbor.) By contrast, if ethics follows Immanuel Kant, biblical commands are read as logically necessary absolute rules. Biblical exhortations based on reward or afterlife then become an embarrassment and are discounted as concessions to self-interest.

Ogletree points out that the predominant moral preunderstanding in our culture today, consequentialism, finds the least support in Scripture. Most of the OT and NT authors could not conceive of the possibility of social experimentation and transformation. He gives priority to a character-based ethics rooted in the relations with God, Christ, and fellow believers. He acknowledges a more limited role for an ethics of principles within the overall ethics of relations. Law can express what the community has settled by negotiation and it can articulate predictable patterns of social life. He writes, "Law and promise are then dialectically related. Law articulates promise, and promise is the underlying basis of law."[21] This combined mode of application retrieves Reformation insights concerning Law and Gospel in a more sophisticated way. It also enables Ogletree to consider a wide range of biblical material relating to morality.

One wonders whether consequential appeals are absent from Scripture. What about the blessings and curses of Deuteronomy or the warnings and promises of the prophets from Amos to Zechariah? The whole of the New Testament is acutely conscious that present behavior has consequences for eternal life or damnation. Many moral philosophers today consider that appeals to rewards and punishments are amoral at best, since they are addressed to self-interest. They hold that these appeals undermine morality because acts should be done or avoided on the basis of their intrinsic moral value and not for extrinsic considerations. At the same time, many mainstream churches do not talk about heaven because they seem embarrassed about hell or the whole possibility of an "afterlife." Nevertheless, the canon of Scripture will not let us ignore these issues, even if our cultural horizon makes them unpalatable.

Like Ogletree, recent Catholic social teachings favor a combined method of application. For example, the United States bishops' statement on the nuclear question invokes biblical visions of peacemaking alongside just war thinking and their document on economic justice combines a biblical description of justice and community with human rights principles.[22] They believe that a biblically informed vision establishes a perspective that highlights certain values, such as the preferential option for the poor, but that vision requires principles of justice like equality and participation to move to policy recommendations. The U.S. bishops work from the explicit assumption that believers and nonbelievers share a common humanity created by God which is the basis of human rights in the public realm. "These rights are bestowed on human beings by God and grounded in the nature and dignity of human persons. They are not created by society."[23]

Sophisticated historical criticism has made many theologians hesitant to cite specific biblical moral norms. The broader categories of biblical story and symbol and the appeal of parable and metaphor seem to travel better from biblical societies to the present. Some deontological methods abstract a timeless moral core from terms and norms, as when Gene Outka argues that mutual regard is the rational moral core of NT *agape*.[24] Others insist that specific NT prescriptions should not be translated into general moral language. Hays writes,

> The interpreter should not turn narratives into law (for instance, arguing that Acts 2:44–45 requires Christians to own all things in common) or rules into principles (e.g., by suggesting that the commandment to sell possessions and give alms [Luke 12:33] is not meant literally but that it points to the principle of inner detachment from our wealth).[25]

The diverse material in Scripture calls for a plurality of methods for selecting, interpreting, and applying the Word of God. Theologians are saying a variety of things about Scripture and ethics and no single approach can do justice to that plurality. Five different ways of using Scripture for moral guidance emerge from reading the wide range of theological positions: Scripture as the command of God, as moral reminder, as call to liberation, as call to discipleship, and as the basis of responding love. These five approaches structure the five chapters of this book. The pluralism in this discussion does not indicate scholarly confusion so much as the irreducible richness of Scripture itself. Believing that four Gospels are better than a single one, the Church welcomed pluralism even in its most central document. Both our moral life and the range of literary forms in the Bible are simply too rich to be reduced to a single moral system.

1
The Command of God

The first model of using Scripture for moral guidance focuses on the experience of the divine call as the paradigm for the Christian's relation to God. God reveals the divine reality in calling particular persons to respond. Only those who obediently accept the call receive the self-disclosure of God. This directive is not a general moral principle but a specific personal invitation which calls for a life decision. In every moral decision, according to this approach, God is the commander and the believer is the one commanded. To the basic moral question "What ought I to do?" there is a direct answer: You should listen to God's command and obey it without question or reservation.

Israel's faith history revolves around these personal calls, beginning with the call of Abram that demands a total response. The mysterious presence summons him to leave his familiar world and "go to a land that I will show you" (Gen 12:1). Every major chapter of Israel's story begins with a similar call. A reluctant Moses is called to lead the people out of slavery by a Lord who will accept no excuses. The prophets speak with the Lord's authority because they have been summoned personally by the Lord. Jesus proclaims the Kingdom as an unequivocal claim on those who hear; some leave everything behind to follow him while others, like the rich young man, turn away.

The paradigm of command emerged most clearly after the First World War in the neo-orthodox movement which sought to undo Protestantism's compromise with modern culture and revive the biblical foundation of faith. The return to a theological ethics based on Scripture alone (*sola Scriptura*) may appear to be an end run around the problems of hermeneutics, a withdrawal from social complexities into individual searching of the Scriptures for guidance. The neo-orthodox were consciously critical of many features of their culture. On the other hand, their conviction that the living God was in active and direct communication with believers obviates some hermeneutical issues. They did not focus on the relation of an ancient text to contemporary problems but on the sovereign Lord whom Scripture witnessed and whose revelation and communication continue into the present. Their return to a more vigorous form of Reformation theology testifies to the important role that reflection on the contemporary world plays in stimulating a fresh reading of the biblical text, in this instance a reading which revised the interpretation of Scripture received from the Lutheran and Reformed traditions. We will first examine Dietrich Bonhoeffer, who graphically exposed the problem in Nazi Germany, and then turn to neo-orthodoxy's main advocate, Karl Barth, who taught Bonhoeffer and influenced him throughout his life.

I. Dietrich Bonhoeffer: The Cost of Discipleship

Bonhoeffer's life is the finest testimony to the soundness of his theology. He wrote *The Cost of Discipleship* in 1937 at the age of thirty-one when he was rector of a seminary for the Confessing Church, which opposed the Nazi-dominated German National Church. The Nazis later imprisoned and executed him on the grounds that he was involved in a plot to assassinate Hitler.

Bonhoeffer staunchly resisted the complacency and silence of European Christianity, especially the German church, in the face of fascism. He articulated Jesus' call to radical discipleship, which demanded wholehearted obedience to the way that leads to the cross. His writings continue to influence Christians who draw a clear line between the Church and secular culture, like the socially active Evangelicals. His book *The Cost of Discipleship* describes Jesus' demanding invitation to his disciples and asserts that the same invitation is extended to us today.[1] The first encounter with Jesus sets the paradigm, the normative pattern, for the life of faith. Jesus demands that the individual leave behind ordinary life and pursue an uncharted path in fellowship with him.

Bonhoeffer's selection of biblical material signals his departure from conventional Lutheran ethics. Unlike its standard focus on the doctrine of justification in Romans and Galatians, he begins with the direct and unconditional calls of Levi, Peter, and the rich young man. "Jesus' summons to the rich young man was calling him to die," writes Bonhoeffer, "because only a man who is dead to his own will can follow Christ. In fact every command of Jesus is a command to die, with all our affections and lusts."[2] He comments at length on Matthew 5 to 7, the Sermon on the Mount, to spell out the particular commands of discipleship, which echo the same stark demand for obedience as the initial encounter. The missionary discourse of Matthew 9 and 10 specifies the conditions for preaching the Gospel and continuing the ministry of Jesus. In order to show how the call to become disciples continues today, he turns to Romans 6 and First Corinthians to argue that the commitment of baptism and life in the Body of Christ make the same demands and offer the same fellowship with Jesus as the call of the first disciples.

Bonhoeffer's revised interpretation of the Lutheran doctrine of Law and Gospel accounts for his unconventional focus on passages that spell out the particular moral demands of following Christ. In the face of German Christianity which had betrayed the Gospel to keep peace with the Third Reich, Bonhoeffer reprimanded his fellow Lutherans for misunderstanding the relationship between Law and Gospel, between faith and works. Martin Luther had been suspicious that every Christian harbored within herself or himself a legalistic Pharisee who would convert the free gift of God's grace into a commercial transaction. Since too much gratuity was threatening, Christians would be tempted to bargain with God by using their good works to purchase God's love. They would try to keep the Law in order to earn the grace of the Gospel; Luther learned from Paul that earned grace was no grace at all. Therefore, he insisted that the path to grace was not the Law but confident surrender to God through the person of Christ.

Luther held that Law had two functions: the "spiritual use of the Law" which pointed out transgressions and so led the individual to despair of attaining grace through good conduct, and the "civil use of the Law" which was simply to restrain the forces of chaos in secular society. Luther had not ignored the call to moral living which was inherent in the promise of the Gospel; he urged Christians to live out the

Gospel by being other "Christs" to the neighbor.[3] Although he paid considerable attention to the lazy believers who used "evangelical freedom" as an excuse to rest on their laurels of justification, he was remembered more for his early polemics against the self-justifying legalists. Over time, many of his followers tended to play down the need for ethics to guide the believer into behavior corresponding to the Christian calling. Luther also favored a dispositional ethic where the real intent of every commandment is to foster certain attitudes in the believer, thereby taking away any opportunity to boast that the commandment has been perfectly observed. Finally, Luther had granted considerable latitude to the state from relying on Paul's counsel in Rom 13:1–6 to respect civil authorities as being God's instrument. Increasingly, this position encouraged many Lutherans to take a passive, uncritical attitude toward civil government.

Bonhoeffer certainly agreed that faith came only by accepting the *free* gift of the promise of Christ, but he insisted that the gift was inseparable from the call to live the way of Jesus. The moral inertia which he witnessed in the German churches was the "cheap grace" of Gospel without Law which contrasts starkly with the costly grace of true discipleship. "Such grace is *costly*," he wrote, "because it calls us to follow, and it is *grace* because it calls us to follow *Jesus Christ*."[4] Cheap grace absolves sins without requiring repentance and enables the Christian to be perfectly at home in the world, even the world of Nazi Germany.

In order to show that faith entails moral fidelity, Bonhoeffer strove to discover a more integral connection between Law and Gospel. When Jesus Christ calls a person, it transcends any distinction between Law and Gospel. He summons us to exclusive attachment to his person; it is thus a gracious summons, not a legal imperative. Nevertheless, one cannot believe without obedient action: "Christ calls, the disciple follows, that is grace and commandment in one."[5] The encounter with the rich young man in Matthew 19 shows this connection. Jesus is not interested in the man's moral quandaries, but in the man himself. When confronted by the summons to discipleship, the young man and all of us face a yes or no choice. Only if he is obedient and follows Jesus down the road can the man enter into that relationship with Jesus in which he may know the mercy and graciousness of God. The young man does have a choice; the call does not suspend his humanity. His obedience will be the first step of faith. He must not wait until he has "sufficient" faith before being obedient; he must take the step. And there is the tragedy: "Because he would not obey, he could not believe."[6] We delude ourselves if we think we must develop more faith before answering the call. "Only he who believes is obedient, and only he who is obedient believes."[7] Bonhoeffer relishes paradox as much as Luther did. Complaining that our faith is insufficient shows that we do not yet have faith; much of our morally earnest questioning is an attempt to dilute the radical summons of Jesus. We do not need to know where the journey of discipleship will lead because it will be uncharted, just as was Abram's. The wandering Aramaean did not know where he was being led, only that he was being led. The obscurity of following the divine summons in faith is so important for Bonhoeffer that he is reluctant to spell out precisely *how* we are to apply the message. Presumably, those who hear will know what to do.

The Cross of Christ as Moral Standard

Every Christian ethics is a careful balance of several components, usually around one dominant theme. In Catholic moral theology, that primary strand was traditionally the natural law philosophical explanation of morality. We will see that the doctrine of God dominates Barth's ethics. James Gustafson showed in his *Christ and the Moral Life* how various Christologies have guided the major thinkers in the Christian tradition.[8] Emphasizing different aspects of belief in Christ shapes the appropriate moral response of the Christian. Jesus Christ plays the central role in Bonhoeffer's interpretation. The command of God leads to closer conformity to Christ. Christ is the Mediator who comes between the Christian and the neighbor and between the disciple and the command because they can be appreciated only through him. His life interprets the command, and it is his personal authority that summons the disciple. If we follow Jesus because the command is a means to personal fulfillment or reward, then we are letting the command come between ourselves and Jesus. Unquestioning obedience is possible not because the command is perfectly rational or attractive, but because the One who gives the command is unconditionally trustworthy.

For Bonhoeffer, the cross is the true measure of Christology in ethics. This traditional Lutheran theme gains added significance from the persecution which faithful Christians could expect from the totalitarian state. Jesus is the image of God, the standard for humanity that overrules any philosophical definition of what it means to be human. Nothing is more revealing of Christ than his sufferings, nothing more definitive for the way of discipleship. "Just as Christ is Christ only in virtue of his suffering and rejection," writes Bonhoeffer, so the disciple "is a disciple only in so far as he shares his Lord's suffering and rejection and crucifixion."[9]

The cross is the sign of contradiction which revolutionizes all our personal values and projects. Bonhoeffer reads the demands of the Sermon on the Mount in paradoxical and provocative ways which allow no room for diluting them with common sense and concessions to human frailty. He agrees with Augustine that human accomplishments and virtues have no value when they are independent of the realities of faith. Each value must be submitted to the unique historical standard of the cross and resurrection of Christ to determine its actual meaning. We cannot presume to know from human experience what God is doing in Christ, as Bonhoeffer eloquently argues in his *Ethics*. He comments on the clause "God is love" from the First Letter of John 4:16:

> First of all, for the sake of clarity, this sentence is to be read with the emphasis on the word God, whereas we have fallen into the habit of emphasizing the word love. *God* is love; that is to say not a human attitude, a conviction or a deed, but God Himself is love. Only he who knows God knows what love is; it is not the other way round; it is not that we first of all by nature know what love is and therefore know also what God is. No one knows God unless God reveals Himself to him. And so no one knows what love is except in the self-revelation of God....Only in Jesus Christ do we know what love is, namely in His deed for us. "Hereby perceive we the love of God, because He laid down His life for us." (I John 3:16)[10]

The New Testament answers the question "What is love?" by pointing directly to the saving deed and person of Jesus Christ. He is the only standard that matters. Philosophical ethics does not get equal time because reason is obscured by sin and cultural blindness. Human experience apart from revelation is suspect here as it is in a number of other theologies coming from the Reformation.

How does the call of Christ get applied to our lives today? How can we know where to find it? Although the person of Christ is central to this schema, discipleship does not imply literal imitation of his public ministry or his poverty. Slavish imitation would evade radical obedience because it would hide behind the biblical text to avoid God's living word that commands us anew. For subsequent generations of Christians, the call to discipleship is contained in their baptismal vocation and in their common life in the Body of Christ. Bonhoeffer does not expect that the Holy Spirit will communicate particular commands to us by some special revelation. "If you would hear the call of Jesus, you need no personal revelation: all you have to do is hear the sermon and receive the sacrament, that is to hear the gospel of Christ crucified and risen. Here he is, the same Christ whom the disciples encountered...."[11] As we shall see below, Bonhoeffer relied on Barth's description of the command of God to a great extent. For both the metaphor of hearing is central: the disciple's responsibility is to hear and obey the command wholeheartedly, not to figure out the mechanics of its transmission.

In *Ethics* Bonhoeffer provides some clarification on the call of discipleship by referring to the claims of family, civic and vocational responsibilities.[12] Traditional Lutheran theology saw these "orders of creation" as provisional indications of the will of God. In this fallen world, God wills that we respond to the demands of family, state and vocation, at least to prevent social chaos. They cannot directly express the command of God, however, since they are inevitably tainted with sin. Like Karl Barth, Bonhoeffer converts moral problems into opportunities for radical faith or radical refusal. They dismiss the usual operations of moral reflection (seeking moral clarity, probing the issue's complexities, weighing competing claims) as tactics for evading the surrender in faith demanded by the command of God. To those believers who object that they do not hear the command of God in such concrete detail, the reply is straightforward: Listen more attentively with a heart ready to obey the Lord.

Karl Barth sounds this same theological polemic against philosophical ethics but he has to modify it when he gets down to treating actual moral issues. Although he thunders against the dangers of ethics for the believer, he makes a number of moral generalizations to clarify the command of God on abortion, war, and capital punishment. It appears that Christian ethics cannot be done on graced intuition alone. Some normative view of humanity, of what we are and what we ought to become, seems necessary when even neo-orthodox theologians get practical.

II. Karl Barth: The Command of God

Karl Barth offers the most thorough theological rationale for using Scripture as the command of God. He strove to redirect the course of Protestant Christianity in this century through strenuous ecclesiastical and political efforts, as well as his monumental *Church Dogmatics* (written from 1925 to 1955). His distrust of compromised Christianity antedates the Nazi era. As a student he had completely accepted his mentors' blend of Christian faith and bourgeois German humanism but the outbreak of World War I shattered this illusion. The young Swiss was scandalized when almost all of his teachers abandoned their socialist and pacifist principles to line up with German nationalism. Their political collapse proved to him that their theological foundations were bankrupt. This experience drove him to rediscover "the Godness of God" and find ways to speak about God that were not compromised by worldly allegiances.

In his groundbreaking *Epistle to the Romans* Barth returned to the theological method he found in Luther and Calvin.[13] Theology must be based on the plain sense of Scripture and dogma should be articulated in order to proclaim the Gospel. Theology could not depend upon any philosophical school because that would make the Gospel the lesser partner and subordinate it to the wisdom of the current culture. The neo-orthodox movement that Barth inspired was a bracing antidote to the blandness of Protestant liberalism and continues to support the cultural critique of evangelicals today. One wonders, however, whether "the plain sense" of Scripture can be grasped in such uninterpreted purity. It is hard to ignore the influence of Augustine's reading of Paul's theology on the writings of the great Reformers.[14] It is equally difficult to miss the role that existentialism played in Barth's ethics of the command of God, even though Barth does not acknowledge this influence. For hermeneutics today, *sola Scriptura* is an impossible ideal, despite Barth's life-long campaign to reinstate it as the standard for theology.

This attempt to ground theology in Scripture did not make Barth a fundamentalist. He articulated the theological principles which guided his interpretation of the Bible, unlike fundamentalists who pretend that they have no theoretical commitments.[15] Barth consciously defended his allegiance to the tradition of Reformed theology which centers on the doctrine of a sovereign and gracious God. (Bonhoeffer was equally candid about his Lutheran commitments which place the crucified Christ at the foundation.) Barth's ethics are unrelentingly *theological* because each discussion of ethics is presented as a corollary of a basic faith affirmation about God. The election of God precedes his treatment of the command of God; the doctrine of divine creation shapes his ethics concerning the protection of life; and God's reconciliation through Christ sets the context for the love command and the specific demands of Christian discipleship. Theology comes before ethics and controls it because Christian moral action is fundamentally a grateful response to what God has done for us in Christ.

Barth's selection of biblical material flows directly from his basic metaphor of moral experience: the command coming from the sovereign divine Commander. Scripture testifies that God deals directly with humans and calls them to very specific actions. Although Barth ranges over much of the canon, the most telling incidents are ones where people are confronted by God's word that interrupts their ordinary lives and demands unconditional obedience to the Commander. The calls of the patriarchs of Israel and the apostles are central while the more mundane morality of wisdom literature and the parables is largely ignored. Christians do not have to examine "the signs of the times" to detect God's will. God's commands are not general moral principles founded on human nature or observation of experience. The one who receives a command does not have to inquire about its content; in fact, asking questions would be the beginning of disobedience. Because commands are direct and definite, the important moral virtues for Barth are attitudes that lead to prompt and wholehearted obedience.

The biblical norm for Christian action cannot be confined to specific prescriptive passages. The overall witness of Scripture provides the formal pattern for Christian response. This witness also specifies the attitudes that shape true obedience. Every moral question is at root a religious decision: "What ought I to do?" cannot be answered piece-meal since it is fundamentally a question about my entire existence vis-à-vis God. As with Bonhoeffer, specific moral decisions reaffirm the original religious assent of faith. "The obedience which the command of God demands of man," Barth writes, "is his decision for Jesus Christ. In each individual decision it is a special form, a repetition and confirmation of this decision."[16] The rich man of Mark 10 (parallel to Bonhoeffer's meditation on Matt 19) disobeys the call to faith because he concentrates on the moral content of the Decalogue's second table. Confident that he has done God's will because he has kept the commandments, he is actually evading the more radical claim that God in Christ makes upon him. "It is required that he should let himself be loved," Barth states. "This is the demand to which he is not equal, to which he is disobedient...."[17]

The Sovereign Divine Commander

The paradigm of command and Commander is the key to interpreting the prescriptive material of the Bible. Ethics errs when it interprets the Decalogue or Sermon on the Mount as an instance of more general human obligations (for example, lying is immoral because it destroys social trust). General natural obligations fail to reflect the uniquely personal God who has intervened in human history. When biblical norms are stated in the form of general obligations, we should read them as summaries of many particular divine commands to people which have been united into a comprehensive demand. Even the Decalogue cannot be reduced to moral generalities. Each commandment is a summary of what God has consistently spoken to God's elect. Action beyond these boundaries is known in advance to be inconsistent with the One who established the covenant of grace.

How can God be sovereignly free and yet morally consistent? If God is bound by the moral law, would a universal legal order be ultimate instead of God? The consistency of morality lies in God rather than in any objective moral order. The faithful person must listen for a command that will be unique and specific to his or her situation. The believer, however, does not stand in an historical vacuum. The commandments continue to be relevant for us today, even though they were addressed to particular people of a different time. "As God speaks in the events of these summaries," explains Barth, "He will always and in all circumstances speak to each individual."[18] Barth asserts both the uniqueness and the consistency of the divine command without any careful attempt to reconcile them.

The Sermon on the Mount should be interpreted like the Decalogue. "Now it is Jesus Himself (as once the God of Moses) who defines, in the form of comprehensive positive and negative directions, the sphere in which He is present with His own, with those whom He has called and will call, the sphere of His care for them and lordship over them." Just as the Decalogue marked off the boundaries of the covenant with Israel, so the arduous demands of the Sermon should be received as notification of the new life which has become possible in Christ. The commands to turn the other cheek and to love those who cannot repay us will seem arduous if we look to our own capacities instead of focusing on God. Barth rather grandly dismisses any doubts about human capability. "The limit of their capacity becomes irrelevant," he states, "when that which Jesus the Lord accomplishes for them occupies the center of the picture which is a norm for their own life's picture.... Grace itself decides what is natural in its own sphere."[19] Our limits do not determine the extent of God's gracious renewal. Christians are invited and demanded to conform their lives to the shape of the new humanity which has become present in Jesus Christ.

Law: The Claim of the Gospel

Before we examine how we discover and apply the command of God, we must note two theological positions that undergird Barth's interpretation, namely his redefinition of Law and Gospel and his doctrine of God. Barth inverted the traditional Protestant reading of Law and Gospel to become "Gospel and Law." He develops Calvin's third use of the law which goes beyond its spiritual and civil functions. For the believer, the primary role of law is to instruct and encourage the life of faith. Law is not an obligation tacked on to the Gospel but an integral part of it. "The Law is completely enclosed in the Gospel.... It is not a foreign element which precedes or only follows it. It is the claim which is addressed to us by the Gospel itself, and as such, the Gospel insofar as it has the form of a claim addressed to us, the Gospel which we cannot really hear except as we obey it."[20] The Gospel claims those whom it graces for a life with a definite shape. Law is the form of the Gospel because the response conforms to the gift and is motivated by gratitude for this gift. Because morality is our joyful correspondence to the action of God in history, the whole story of Scripture has moral relevance.

In Barth's theology the experience and theoretical reflection of faith is consistently shaped by the reality of God, not human structures. We experience the moral claim as unconditional, good, and holy because it comes from One who is absolute, good, and holy. We cannot account for these inherent qualities of moral obligation by beginning from the human side. Human nature or the demands of rationality cannot account for the unconditional character of morality. Only a theological account that is genuinely centered on God can explain the qualities of moral obligation. Indeed, every quality of the moral demand points to the divine source. Its goodness is borrowed from the One who issues it. Its uniqueness and singularity reflect the particularity of God. We can discern which moral claims come from God because they are marked by qualities that point back to their divine source. They are unconditional, majestic, right, good, personal, definite, eternal and unifying because they come from the God who has manifested these qualities in the history of salvation.

Obeying the Command of God

Scripture provides *summaries* of God's commands, *attitudes* that should inform our obedience, and *directions* of freedom inherent in the gift itself. It is not a collection of timeless divine rules. The whole of Scripture provides the shape to which our lives should correspond. (As we shall see in the last two chapters, the "story" of Scripture provides the normative framework to hold in proper balance the various attitudes and directions that guide obedience to the divine command.) Against this biblical background we discover God's specific commands in our daily obligations. Those that manifest the gracious qualities evident in the events of salvation will reveal the gracious Commander.

These commands are not bolts out of the blue because "the claim of God's command always wears the garment of another claim."[21] Since we all face numerous claims daily, we must discern which ones come from God by attending to the type of claim they make upon us. Barth offers two principal criteria:

1. The divine command is permission before it is command. It corresponds to the central quality that God has manifested in history, namely, graciousness. Divine commands will be experienced primarily as positive gifts rather than obligations.[22] Gracious permission enables our response by granting us the freedom to *be* in a specific direction. The grace that rules and commands is first of all grace. Commands that are not from God bind us and we experience their bidding as essentially forbidding.

2. The divine command always directs us toward imitation of Jesus Christ because he is the pre-eminent and definitive manifestation of God's grace. We are commanded to take the right *attitude* toward him. "What is required of us," states Barth, "is that our action should be brought into conformity with His action."[23] We are to imitate Jesus in the attitudes of our response rather than in copying the details of the historical Jesus' lifestyle. The self-emptying of Christ (Phil 2:5–11) presents the basic pattern to be imitated. Like Bonhoeffer, Barth avoids specifying the content of Christian ethics; instead he points us to the formal pattern of Christ's life.

In the final section of his theological ethics in IV/2 of the *Church Dogmatics*, Barth sets down definite attitudes and even norms for Christian guidance. The Spirit of Jesus can be expected to lead the Christian in definite directions that correspond to the witness of Jesus: indifference toward possessions and worldly honors, renunciation of force, dissolution of familial attachments, freedom from self-justifying religion, and the overriding directive to take up the cross.[24]

Is this ethics of the command of God a form of moral intuitionism, where private inspirations are not accountable to rational standards? The answer lies in Barth's discussion of the divine command to respect and protect life, found in *Church Dogmatics* III/4.[25] The "prominent lines" of God's commanding turn out to be fairly definite in practice. Without abandoning his polemic against ethical reflection Barth outlines moral norms and their legitimate exceptions on questions of abortion, suicide, capital punishment, self-defense, war, and mercy killing.

Before describing the Law concerning the protection of life, Barth proclaims the divine gift of the Gospel. "The *real* truth is not that we must live," he states. "It is that we may live. Life is the freedom which is bestowed by God."[26] The doctrine of creation teaches that life is a blessing, a loan from God of something that belongs to God. Consequently, the claim of Law inheres in the theological content of the Gospel: we must treat our own existence and that of others with respect and joy. Since we are created for freedom in fellowship with others as well as with God, the gift of life entails social obligations.

This theology of obligation interprets the commandment "Thou shalt not kill." It forbids murder, not every taking of human life. Barth states general norms for deciding life and death issues. There are legitimate exceptions to each of these norms except the prohibition against mercy-killing. God, the Lord of life, would never command it. Listening for the command of God seems to involve the very moral reflection which he had earlier derided. The judgment of God decides, states Barth, "which in the last analysis we must all hear in every actual or conceivable situation after considering the human arguments on both sides."[27]

The command to protect life usually forbids taking life in abortion, but not always. "Let us be quite frank," writes Barth, "and say that there are situations in which the killing of germinating life does not constitute murder but is in fact commanded."[28] When the pregnant woman's life is tragically threatened by the fetus, then a legitimate exception can be made to the general command to protect life.

Killing in self-defense remains highly suspect due to the Gospel prohibitions against it. They bind the Christian to greater respect for the opponent's life than what is required naturally. The New Testament sayings on non-resistance do not merely "constitute a special rule for good or particularly good Christians. They declare the simple command of God which is valid for all men in its basic and primary sense, and which is thus to be kept until further notice." Although he criticizes Tolstoy and Gandhi for making an absolute prohibition against killing in self-defense, Barth concedes that they are closer to Jesus' attitude than "the primitive gospel of the mailed fist and all the doctrines that have tried to blunt the edge of these sayings."[29]

Barth wrestles with the case of his friend and former student, Bonhoeffer. How could a faithful Christian pacifist be justified in plotting to kill Hitler? If the plotters did receive a clear command from God, why did they not act in full disregard for their own lives so the deed could be done? Standing outside their dialogue with God, Barth cannot resolve the issue: "The only lesson to be learned is that they had no clear and categorical command from God to do it. Otherwise they would have had to overcome what was not in any case an ethical difficulty.... In such a situation it might well have been the command of God. For all we know, perhaps it was, and they failed to hear it."[30] Barth's puzzlement exposes the problems of intuitionism that linger in this model of ethics. In difficult or tragic moral cases, only those who hear the command can know whether an action is justified or not. They cannot convince others who do not hear the same command of God that they are right, and no investigation of the results can indicate whether they acted morally or not.

Few theologians have portrayed the drama of human engagement with God—or rather God's engagement with us—so vividly as Karl Barth. Nevertheless, one must admit that something is missing from this theological ethics. The human partner in the dialogue remains sketchy, fluid, undefined. The moral agent becomes real only when addressed by the Word of God. Moral agents seem to acquire a unique history and moral responsibility only insofar as they are constantly addressed by God. Barth refuses to pay attention to the self apart from God's direct communication. What happens to the moral agent in between the moments when God is commanding? Moral life encompasses more than discrete moments of decision; it refers also to the continuous and enduring aspects which define the self: commitments and roles, virtues and vices, memory, identity and character. Even if one holds on theological grounds that the assent of faith is more fundamental than moral reflection, Barth seems to have maximized the role of obedient faith at the expense of a coherent sense of the moral self.

Does the command of God model still have much influence in theology today? Neo-orthodoxy had a bracing impact on Protestant theology, but faded from the mainstream since mid-century. Although Reinhold and H. Richard Niebuhr benefitted from neo-orthodoxy's critique of cultural Christianity, they developed ethical approaches which relied on human reflection rather than on direct commands from God. Bonhoeffer's *The Cost of Discipleship* became one of the classics of twentieth century spirituality and continues to inspire counter-cultural movements like the Catholic Workers and communities of socially active Evangelicals. Mainstream Protestant theologians have shifted their attention to the human agent and social institutions instead of referring every issue to the doctrine of God. Barth has been appropriated by more conservative evangelical Christians like the Dutch Reformed, who have modified the intuitionist dimensions of his ethics.

Richard J. Mouw mounts a philosophically informed defense of divine command ethics, although he sees the directives more as moral principles rather than personal inspirations. Mouw argues against dismissing an ethics of obedience to God as "heteronomous," that is, abdicating moral responsibility by submitting to an external directive. The alternative to an infantile heteronomy is not necessarily complete moral autonomy where the agent is responsible only to reason. Christians do not believe they are God's equals; God is morally superior and has a unique authority which is based more on love and compas-sionate involvement with humans than on metaphysical status. Mouw writes, "Whether a given individual possesses the authority to command our obedience is a matter which must be decided by examining the credentials of the would-be commander. In this regard it is important to note that the God of Scriptures regularly offers credentials for our examination."[31] Although Calvinism runs the risk of conceiving God as a solitary and even arbitrary monarch, it counters that risk by "viewing the omnipotent Sovereign as immersed in lawlike consistency and covenantal fidelity."[32] Mouw is more willing than Barth to investigate the consistency of human moral experience, recognizing the contribu-tion of narrative to forming moral character and the need for rational reflection and discernment even on the part of those who are open to hear the divine commands.

Donald G. Bloesch relies heavily on Barth for his evangelical systematic theology and ethics. He accepts the reversal of Law and Gospel to Gospel and Law as a major step forward in the Reformed tradition. Nevertheless, he believes that Barth underestimated the remaining tension between Law and Gospel: "we must insist that it remains a commandment even while it may also be heard as permission."[33] Obedience to God's summons does not transform the natural makeup of the moral agent since God's will always stands in tension with natural desires and social expectations. In applying faith to practice, however, Bloesch concedes a greater role for various forms of moral insight than Barth did. "The situation is not a norm for our decision, but it is the field in which our decision takes place.... God's commandment is absolute, but our perception and formulation of it is relative.... In an ethical decision we must take into consideration motives and consequences, but we do not base our decision on these alone, or even on these primarily."[34] Although Bloesch seems more confident than Mouw that the command of God is frequently addressed in quite specific ways to particular persons, both acknowledge that moral reflection plays an integral role in faithful obedience.

In the strongest forms of the command of God model, the moral life remains a sporadic affair. Although Barth restored the normative and dispositional resources to Christian ethics that his more existentialist allies, Rudolf Bultmann and Emil Brunner, wanted to banish, nevertheless the moral agent seems curiously underdeveloped. Is the sovereign God diminished by admitting that humans develop virtues, moral character, and critical capacities for analyzing their situations and making reflective decisions even when they are not inspired? We must pay attention to additional biblical material in order to redress the imbalance of this existential model of call and response. The next chapter will show how the continuous features of human existence— nature, reason, role-obligations—ground a very different Christian ethics of natural law that also finds support in the diverse canon of Scripture.

2
Scripture as Moral Reminder

Our second approach to the use of Scripture in ethics comes from a different theological universe than the command of God model. There is not the stark contrast between nature and grace, ethics and revelation, because grace restores human nature to what God intended it to be and revelation reminds us of morality which is integrally human. Scripture is not full of paradoxical commands but offers the power to do what we know to be right but find ourselves incapable of doing.

This more humanistic approach answers the question "What ought I to do?" with the advice, "Be human, as God created you to be and as Christ has empowered you to be." God's will for humanity was structured into our innermost drives at the creation and sin has not eradicated that design. Humans can recognize God's plan by rational reflection without explicit revelation. The redemptive grace of Christ heals a wounded humanity which never completely lost its status as image of God. The Gospel, therefore, does not ask us to reject our humanity but empowers us to flourish in the way that God originally intended. Whenever we recognize what acts and values lead to human flourishing, we are discovering the will of God for us, since fundamentally God intends that we live fully and humanely. Scripture *reminds us* what it means to be human and calls us to live an integral human life that our egotism would ignore. While God may in some exceptional instances immediately command certain individuals to do something, usually God works through various human media: reason informed by virtue, culture, practical experience, and the best of human wisdom. For Barth and Bonhoeffer, these sources were so distorted by sin that Scripture provided the only trustworthy moral resource.

Every theological ethics begins from one of the four sources of Christian ethics: Scripture, tradition, ethics, and pertinent empirical data. The "moral reminder" approach begins from ethics, the theory of what is normatively human. A particular form of ethics, natural law, controls its use of the other sources. Roman Catholic moral theology looks like the mirror image of Barth, who centered on particular directives communicated from the sovereign God to individuals. For centuries moral theology started with general moral principles and confidently applied them to particular cases, usually without any reference to Scripture. The discipline of moral theology was a practical one geared to training priests to hear the confessions of Catholics and help them assess what their sins were in order to receive sacramental absolution. It concentrated on acts, intentions, and circumstances which defined the nature and gravity of sin. The older moral theology operated in a theological vacuum, virtually untouched by any reference to Christ, the role of the Spirit, sanctification, or discipleship. These matters were assumed to be covered in other branches of theology or spirituality. The religious neutrality of natural law ethics has a positive side in that it can address social issues in a language that can make sense to believers and nonbelievers alike because it appeals to common human values and principles. On the negative side, a natural law that bracketed religious convictions denigrated a distinctively Christian faith vision because it failed to connect the consciences of believers to the religious realities which are the wellsprings of Christian motivation and commitment.

We will examine the renewal of moral theology in the past genertion particularly through the writings of Josef Fuchs, who is the key figure in this transformation. Fuchs is a German Jesuit priest who has taught for many years at the Gregorian University in Rome.[1] With Bruno Schüller, Peter Knauer, Richard A. McCormick, and others, Fuchs developed the school known as "autonomy ethics" which combines a humanistic ethics with the theology of grace proposed by Karl Rahner, the foremost Catholic theologian of this century. This school has been criticized by younger theologians such as Vincent MacNamara and by more conservative official voices like Cardinal Josef Ratzinger and Pope John Paul II in his recent encyclical "The Splendor of Truth."[2]

I. Natural Morality in Scripture

Natural law thinkers appeal to Scripture to underwrite their humanistic and empirical approach to ethics. There are many biblical passages and literary genres that presume some natural human morality in their audience. Scripture itself does not claim to be the only source of morality. Wisdom literature draws on the common observations of the sages about human experience; in some places it endorses their insights by appealing to the principle of divine Wisdom which operates in creation apart from any explicit revelation. The prophets condemn the foes of Israel for greed, injustice, and oppression which they should have known were immoral. The New Testament seems even more open to secular moral wisdom, possibly because the Jewish world had become more cosmopolitan under Hellenistic and Roman influences. Jesus frequently taught in parables which make no mention of God or revelation. They focus on the ordinary world of women who lose coins, sons who leave home, workers who complain about their wages, clever stewards who know how to cut a deal, and irate masters who want a return on their investments. These mundane settings are clues to the gracious action of God; they are not amoral or opaquely "secular."

Paul and the pastoral epistles reach out even more to other sources to make the Good News intelligible to gentile converts. Lists of virtues and vices are borrowed from the surrounding culture (I Cor 6:9–11; Rom 1:29–31; Gal 5:19–21). Christians are exhorted to measure up to the moral standards of their pagan neighbors—which presumes that the gentiles have some capacity for morality (1 Cor 10:32; 1 Thess 4:12; Col 4:5; 1 Pet 2:12, 15; 3:1, 16). Paul exhorts the Philippians to be expansive in learning from the best that humanity has to offer: "whatever is true, whatever is honorable, whatever is just, whatever is pure, whatever is lovely, whatever is gracious, if there is any excellence and if there is anything worthy of praise, think about these things." (Phil 4:8)

The first two chapters of Romans provide the classical warrant for natural law theology. They contain a moral preunderstanding that every human being has the capacity to tell moral right from moral wrong. Although Paul does not mention moral norms in his diatribe against the pagans in 1:18–32, he presumes that nature offers sufficient testimony to the existence of God and to appropriate human conduct. The pagans are culpable for violating God's unconditional claim on them by refusing to believe and by acting licentiously.[3] The second chapter makes this position more explicit. The Jews will be condemned because they had the Law of Moses and ignored it. The gentiles are also accountable, even though they did not have the revealed law:

> They are a law for themselves even though they do not have the law. They show that the demands of the law are written in their hearts, while their conscience also bears witness and their conflicting thoughts accuse and defend them...(2:14–15).

These arguments lead up to the conclusion in 3:22 that gentiles and Jews have all sinned and fallen short of the glory of God; therefore, all humanity stands in need of the redemption of Christ. This theological conclusion rests on a moral assumption. The universal state of sin presumes some universal moral standards in the conscience of every person, whether they are stipulated in revelation or simply part of common human experience. Schüller judges that most major exegetes of Romans today, both Protestant and Catholic, "interpret the texts in question in the sense of a natural law."[4]

Paul teaches elsewhere that Scripture is not the only source of moral knowledge. The grace of Christ consists primarily in the power to do what is right rather than in instruction concerning what is right and wrong for humans. Paul and other NT authors presume or assert that there is a natural moral capacity apart from revelation which has not been erased by sin; they do not explain why this is so. Moral theology, abhorring this vacuum, rushed in with a complex theological rationale to interpret these texts. One gets the impression that these interpretations are guided to a great extent by the moral philosophy which was assumed as a preunderstanding. A natural law tradition which can be traced back to Aristotle and the Stoics was retrieved by Thomas Aquinas in a sophisticated vision which still seems plausible to many Christians seven centuries and at least one Reformation later.

Theological Support for Naturalist Ethics

Ethical naturalism bases moral value and obligation in empirical observations: the "ought" is derived from the "is." As one form of naturalism, natural law ethics argues that moral obligation arises out of our common quest to grow into full humanity. It examines the human person as a developing entity to decide what is moral. Those actions and values that lead to human flourishing, which reasonably enhance individual and communal existence, are judged to be moral. Those which frustrate and diminish integral human development are by that fact immoral. Virtues are skills for living humanely and reasonably; vices are irrational because they cripple human development. Just as every school of psychology has some notion of health that serves as the criterion for its techniques, so too every system of ethics presumes some vision of human flourishing. Granted that psychologists and ethicists will disagree on what constitutes full human living, they necessarily presume some model in their arguments. The noted Anglican theologian John Macquarrie writes that "natural law is foundational to morality. It is the inner drive toward authentic person-hood and is presupposed in all particular ethical traditions, including the Christian one."[5] Natural law claims to be objective rather than arbitrary because morality is not established by social convention or by legislation of the powerful. It is objective because it rests on a given— "the inner drive toward authentic personhood."

Natural law uses the term "law" in an analogous fashion. There is no "code of natural law" which we can consult when solving moral quandaries. It is a process of reflection rather than the codified results of such reflection. Our common human nature functions as a norm or basic "law" because it regulates our conduct. When we judge that certain conduct fosters important human values and a just society and other behavior necessarily erodes them, we have reasonably concluded what is moral. Reason, guided by virtuous habits and grounded in sound empirical observation, is the basis of moral judgment. Human reason must try to reconcile the basic drives and the requirements of living together to discern the appropriate practical action. Reason must be guided by sound inclinations or virtues in order to be consistent and accurate in its reflection. Virtues humanize our basic drives. Courage, prudence, justice and temperance are all necessary to perceive the courageous, prudent, and fair course of action. It takes not only intelligence but virtue to develop social policies that balance freedom and equality, as the debate on affirmative action attests. Although natural law does not guarantee unanimity on such intricate questions, it does provide a common starting point for the debate that is rooted in the humanity of all participants.

In the past two centuries, however, increasing awareness of the great variety of cultures makes many people skeptical that there is a common human nature or universal morality. The natural law traditions have not held that nature operates in a universally uniform way. To cite the analogy of computers, nature is the common hardware which always requires the particular software of culture in order to work. For instance, every human group must have a complex and fairly stable process to raise children. The need for some family structure is natural but the particular culture specifies the form: the institution can be matrilineal, patrilineal, extended family or any number of other configurations. Culture often becomes "second nature" so that we come to presume that the mores of our group must be the norm for all humans. Therefore, the persistent challenge for natural law thinkers is to distinguish what is natural from what is merely cultural.

Naturalist Ethics and Scripture

What does an empirical approach to morality need from theology or Scripture? Mostly it finds corroboration and motivation in religion for natural morality, or a new context for the same obligations and values. Scripture provides *motivation* for moral living but not *content*—that is already given in our humanity. The Bible does not dictate morality since that is determined from observing human experience. Jesus does not proclaim a new morality but restores the values that God intended from the beginning. Take the case of divorce. In Matthew 19 Jesus shocks his audience by asserting that marriage cannot be dissolved. Moses' permission of divorce was a concession to the Israelites' hard hearts but it was not what God intended from the beginning, which is why Genesis mandates that "the two shall become one flesh" (Gen 2:24). Barth based the permanence of marriage on the covenant fidelity of God which Christians are permitted and commanded to witness. The natural law tradition, by contrast, asserts that the objective human reality of marriage demands its permanence. Even those who do not accept a divine creation should be able to see that a permanent loving marriage is the optimal context for human intimacy and raising children. The ought (the obligation to permanence) arises from the is (the human condition of marriage and family as adequately considered).

Scripture can give theological warrants, or backing, for this humanistic ethics primarily through the doctrines of creation and incarnation. The "givenness" of human values and obligations comes from God's designs in creation. In the event of the incarnation, the Son of God embraces humanity and restores it to God's original intentions. Josef Fuchs in his book *Natural Law: A Theological Investigation*, clarified the theological foundations of natural law in response to the charges of Barth and Emil Brunner that it was naive about human sinfulness and minimized the saving work of Christ.[6] Catholic theology holds for a humanity that images God even after the Fall because sinners still retain the imprint of God in their capacity to know the truth and choose the good, even though the intellect is darkened and the will weakened by sin.

Fuchs points to the great Christological hymns that are prologue to John's gospel and the letters to the Ephesians and Colossians to negate the charge that natural law ethics relies on creation rather than the redemption of Christ. All things, and especially humanity, were created in Christ and for Christ; therefore, nature from the beginning is oriented to find its full meaning in Christ. The Incarnation is not an afterthought or only a remedy for sin, because the union of God and humanity in Christ was intended from the beginning. Nature is not the enemy of grace but the condition for the possibility of God's self-communication in history. Since humans are designed to be "hearers of the Word," (as Karl Rahner expressed it), nature is the other who is meant to receive God's love. Therefore, we should expect some continuity between the Word and its addressee.

While it is obvious that we never experience nature as unaffected by sin, it is also true, if less obvious, that we do not experience nature as untouched by God's grace. Fuchs and many other Catholic thinkers rely on Karl Rahner's theology which holds that grace pervades natural experience. Every person is constantly being called by God, even if he or she refuses the invitations. No one can know—or meet—the demands of morality without the assistance of grace, even if the person does not recognize it as grace. Rahner's theory of grace addresses one of the major puzzles to contemporary believers: how can some religiously indifferent people live exemplary, even heroic, moral lives? As they strive to follow the light of conscience they are being supported by the grace of God and are "anonymously" responding to God's reality. Therefore, traditional and more recent natural law theologians have held that one does not have to be religious or Christian in order to be moral. What difference does Christian faith make in living morally? As we shall see, that is the harder question for more humanistic theological ethicists to answer.

The figure of Jesus Christ in this theology is not the sign of contradiction which he is for many theologians shaped by the Reformation. He is the prototype of humanity rather than an alien figure. When his moral teaching is interpreted through the lenses of creation and the incarnation rather than through the cross, its reasonableness comes to the fore, not its paradoxical character which Bonhoeffer insisted upon. Jesus Christ shows in himself what true humanity is meant to be and empowers the Christian to live this full humanity. He does not impose any new moral burdens on his disciples. If some of his teaching seems irrational it is because we have been deceived by sin.

II. Christian Motivation and Human Moral Content

What difference does Christian faith make in the moral life? During the past two decades, Catholic moral theologians debated the question whether there is a distinctive Christian ethics. One group answered affirmatively and became known as "the faith ethics" school. The majority denied that revelation added anything new to ethics, which is independently grounded in nature; hence they were dubbed "the autonomy school." These theologians make little mention of the New Testament's metaphors of radical transformation: moving from darkness to light, slavery to freedom, and death to life. They appeal to the most authoritative voice in the Catholic tradition. Thomas Aquinas held the new "law of Christ" is primarily the gift of the Holy Spirit, and secondarily the written law of biblical revelation. The Spirit gives the person a new "heart" which transforms moral motivation. This gift enables the Christian to desire what is good and accomplish it with ease and delight. The written law does not impose any obligations that were not always part of natural law.[7] Put in contemporary terms, the grace of Christ adds no new *content* to the moral law but a profound new *motivation*, or Christian intentionality. The gift of the Spirit finds practical expression primarily in the virtues of the Christian life, to which Aquinas devotes much more attention than he does to moral norms. Since the written law is secondary to the gift of the Spirit, it should not be the prime focus of moral theology. Fuchs writes about the NT: "Explicit guidance is not a theme of Christian proclamation."[8]

The Gospel presupposes that its hearers know what is morally right even without explicit revelation. When Paul composed his most extended treatment of moral problems in 1 Cor 6 and 7, he is not expressing new moral truths but spelling out how the Corinthians' commitment to Christ should motivate their behavior. Believers "possess a new 'Christian' meaning, a new intentionality, a new and deepened insight into Christian anthropology and ethics, a new motivation for action and a new readiness to live seriously." Their belonging to Christ, which is made possible by the gift of the Holy Spirit, gives them a basic Christian orientation. At the same time, "they must decide which innerworldly behavior is or can be an expression of the biblical orientation."[9] This is precisely the task Paul faces in the Corinthian community. Even where there was a well known saying of Jesus forbidding divorce, the community still had to interpret it (1 Cor 7:8–15). In the new context of Hellenistic marriage practices, a woman could separate from her husband. The new setting raised problems which were not foreseen in the Palestinian context, so "Jesus' words are by themselves, insufficient in the diverse circumstances of life.... Paul does not understand Jesus' words legalistically.... Paul knows that he is capable of discovering solutions for right conduct that are materially reasonable and correspond to the Spirit of Christ."[10] Catholic natural law thinkers have historically been confident not only in human reason but also in an inspired community leadership which would continue to act as the apostles in adapting the message of Jesus to new settings.

The autonomy school distinguishes *moral teaching* that establishes the truth of a moral statement from *moral exhortation* (also called "paranesis") that provides motivation for what is already understood to be moral. Paul's treatment of fornication in 1 Cor 6:12–20 shows the difference. He does not cite religious arguments to prove the immorality of fornication (some libertine converts were frequenting the pagan temple prostitutes). According to Fuchs, Paul "only exhorts them (paranesis) to avoid as Christians what is in any case immoral. In this paranesis, however, he employs a specifically Christian motivation to show a specific unfittingness of fornication—the moral wrongness of which is presupposed—for Christians."[11] For the autonomy school most of what is distinctively Christian in biblical moral texts does not count as moral teaching but as exhortation or paranesis. In fact, Schüller states that Christians should not accept biblical mandates because they are part of revelation but because they are valid in themselves. "To the extent that the word of revelation does contain individual precepts of the law of Christ, it probably intends to help people out at those points where they have not yet managed to apprehend moral precepts on their intrinsic grounds. Even if human beings should never manage to dispense with this assistance totally, nonetheless they should strive to require it as little as possible."[12] Thomas Aquinas, by contrast, thought that biblical revelation of the moral law was a considerable help to humans, most of whom would have arrived at its moral insights only rarely and after considerable struggle.[13]

One wonders if we can be so philosophical as Schüller is about having recourse to Scripture. Does not the very content of some biblical commands seem to go beyond the call of duty? Consider the mandates to love your enemies, take up the cross daily, turn the other cheek, love without thought of return. Would these seem reasonable to a good person who was not guided by allegiance to Jesus of Nazareth and moved by his Spirit? The hard sayings of Jesus appear to have a heroic character that transcends common sense morality. What about the command to take up the cross and follow Jesus, which was the paradigmatic call for Bonhoeffer? Does every natural morality contain the cost of discipleship? Fuchs argues that every serious moral existence involves considerable renunciation, which forces the agent to a self-transcendence that is liable to be costly. Non-Christians and atheists "too experience their egoism as 'fallen' men and are able to understand that in this situation renunciation and self-denial, hence the cross, may be part of authentic being-human."[14] However, only those who know the full story of fallen humanity and the redemption that comes through the cross and resurrection of Jesus Christ can comprehend the full depth of the Christian doctrine of the cross. It is not obvious to me that the command to bear the cross can be abstracted from the personal story of Jesus of Nazareth. Jesus did not only say, "Take up your cross daily," but immediately added "and follow me." The meaning of the cross cannot be separated from the life of discipleship to this particular person. As Bonhoeffer said, Jesus stands between the disciple and the costly demand, thereby altering its meaning.

The theologian who uses Scripture as a moral reminder is not bound by particular mandates which can now be seen as timebound applications of the Gospel. Since this model has a high confidence in human reason and a willingness to consult various sources of human wisdom, it has greater flexibility in fashioning new approaches than ethical models that depend more directly on the canonical text. Although some proponents of natural law have been unwilling to admit that human nature itself changes through time, more historically minded interpreters hold that nature develops through history and morality changes accordingly. Some of the institutions that were considered "natural" in biblical times, like the patriarchal household or slavery, make no moral claim on us today; indeed they seem morally objectionable if not scandalous. Since human nature has grown beyond them, the concrete injunctions about those institutions are irrelevant. The standards for particular moral acts will change as human nature and institutions change. "Absolutes" will be found on the level of values and attitudes rather than in unvarying moral norms that are applicable without exception. Recent papal documents, however, portray human nature as more permanent, thereby providing a foundation for permanent, unexceptional moral norms.

III. Challenges to Autonomous Christian Ethics

Two significant challenges to the autonomy school have appeared recently. The first set of critics questions the philosophical adequacy of the sharp division between religion and morality and between motivation and content. A broader definition of ethics would incorporate more distinctively Christian materials into the content of moral value and obligation. The second set of critics comes from the "faith ethics" school, most notably Pope John Paul II and Cardinal Josef Ratzinger. They insist that the autonomy school has divorced moral reflection from the resources of Scripture and faith, especially as they are defined by the authority of the Church.

A. Philosophical Challenges

Vincent MacNamara mounts a powerful critique of the philosophical preunderstandings and methods of the autonomy school on three matters: the definition of ethics, the distinction of motivation and content, and the status of moral ideals in Christianity.

1. Does Christian experience keep morality and religion in such neatly divided compartments as has been described above? The problem may be a narrow *definition of ethics* that begs the question. A model of ethics which concentrates on duty and the rational application of universal principles has already excluded by definition much of what Scripture has to offer. MacNamara writes,

> But if morality is a matter of virtue and character, if attitudes and innermost desires are important to it and not only observable acts, there is greater room for the claim that there is a specifically Christian morality. The insight of the early church that the Christian should live his life in joy (2 Cor. 9:7; Heb. 10:34), in thankfulness (Acts 5:41; Col. 3:17), in humility (John 13:14–15; Phil. 2:3) and without anxiety (Matt. 6:25; 1 Pet. 5:7) may not lead to an observable difference of behaviour but may refer to attitudes and disposition that are part of Christian virtue.[15]

A more comprehensive model of ethics would also make room for the influence of the moral agent's world-view and the stories that have shaped his or her identity.

2. MacNamara argues rather convincingly that there is considerable confusion in the distinction between *religious motivation and autonomous moral content*. "There are some considerations mentioned by them under the rubric of motive which are really justifying reasons for moral judgment." For instance, Fuchs holds that Christianity provides a motive for virginity by giving one the desire for it, but is that accurate? "Christianity may indeed give the desire for virginity. But, basically, it gives one the reason why virginity is a morally good choice. Without the considerations arising from Christian belief, it might not be an intelligible choice."[16] Christian belief likewise supplies the reasons that morally justify the practices of voluntary poverty, self-sacrifice,

and non-resistance. Faith cannot be relegated to motivating acts whose moral content is fully established on natural grounds. If by "content" we mean "how the act is to be described or characterized," then reasons and intentions supplied by faith enter into the content of many acts. When a Christian and a non-Christian both practice voluntary poverty, is it the same act done from different motives, or are they different acts? MacNamara believes that they are different acts because acts cannot be morally defined on their observable features alone. "*What* is being done is sometimes discovered by asking why it is done. It may well be here that Christian considerations enter: if so, they are more central to morality than the autonomy school allows."[17]

3. The status of *moral ideals in Christian life* marks another distinctive difference from purely natural morality. Because moral ideals cannot be universalized for all rational persons, they are not usually considered to be matters of duty. Generally speaking, people admire those who aspire to such heights but do not blame the rest of humanity for not doing so. MacNamara writes, "Christianity does not regard biblical ideals in the same light in which secular ethics regards ideals.... It does not regard a life of high agape as a matter of choice, as some philosophers do."[18] So even when moral ideals seem to provide a common ground between Christians and non-Christians, those ideals do not make the same moral claim in both groups. Therefore, there is another significant difference between a distinctively Christian ethics and a purely secular one. In the Sermon on the Mount Jesus is not only contrasting full human morality with the practices of fallen humanity but, even more, he is calling all his disciples to a life "above and beyond the call of duty."

Philosopher James Gaffney also argues against Schüller's proposal that biblical moral material should be considered not morally normative but only motivational on account of its exhortative, commendatory element. He points out that an increasing number of moral philosophers today recognize an affective dimension in every statement of moral principle. Content and motivation are inextricably bound up together. When the autonomy school separates the exhortative dimension of biblical moral discourse from its normative, rational element, it makes the same mistake as the philosophical naturalists. "For every ethical norm is parenetic, both intrinsically and reductively. To look for nonparanetic norms on which all parenesis depends is only the notoriously futile quest for some 'is' on which all 'oughts' depend.... On the other hand...pure parenesis is pure moral vapor."[19] Moral principles and judgments simultaneously evaluate and commend their content. For example, when I say, "Justice demands that equals should be treated equally," I am commending the same attitude and conclusion to the audience. The terms "justice" and "equals" are not rhetorically neutral since they are meant to encourage the listeners to adopt the same standard of justice.

Schüller has responded to his critics by qualifying his position on the identity of moral content in religious and nonreligious frameworks. He did not mean that similar norms had exactly the same meaning in both contexts. Their meaning is not univocal but analogous in the different contexts. He writes that "both the law of Christ and the natural law command love of neighbor. But in accordance with its essence the natural law can impose as a duty only a purely human (natural) love of neighbor, whereas the law of Christ commands a love of neighbor which surpasses all human capability, a supernatural love of neighbor."[20] Some might read that as amounting to a difference of content, but Schüller will not concede that point because to do so might erode the rational content of Christian love. Although the autonomy school has far surpassed the older manualist moral theology in validating a religious dimension to the moral life, their sum total usually seems less than the whole of Christian experience. They seem to quarantine the influence of Christian resources in the interest of keeping a common moral ground with nonbelievers and maintaining an intelligible, universally valid center to the moral life. It may be that seeking the family resemblance between different moralities could preserve their distinctiveness without succumbing to relativism which acknowledges no common ground.

B. The "Faith Ethics" Challenge

The second challenge to autonomy ethics comes from the "faith ethics" school, whose approach informs Pope John Paul II's 1993 encyclical, *The Splendor of Truth*. It strongly criticizes what it takes to be the position of the autonomy school and counters by asserting the religious foundations of Christian morality more than any previous papal teaching.[21] The Pope combines a strong affirmation of a universal, objectivist ethics with an equally vigorous insistence that Jesus taught a distinctive ethics for Christians. Biblical ethics is interpreted through a doctrine of Church authority which makes the official Church the privileged teacher of Scripture to subsequent generations. The authoritative *magisterium* takes the place of the historical Jesus since it has been commissioned by the risen Lord to teach in his stead.

The Pope asserts that Christian morality has a distinctive content which is summed up in following Christ in loving service and obedience. He begins with the dialogue between Jesus and the rich young man in Matthew 19 where the moral content of the commandments is reaffirmed as part of discipleship. This encounter locates morality in the more fundamental response to God and the neighbor in love, a response of love and gratitude for "the many gratuitous initiatives taken by God out of love for [us]" (par 10). The moral quest is inseparable from religious realities because whenever we wrestle with the deepest meaning of our life, we are seeking for God. Our longing for the good is radically longing for God, who is the transcendent, personal source of truth and goodness.

Taking the Christian moral path means not only obedience to the commandments, but "**holding fast to the very person of Jesus**, partaking of his life and his destiny, sharing in his free and loving obedience to the will of the Father" (19). The Pope writes that the central commandment of the Christian life is the new commandment of John 13:14–15, 34–35: "Love one another, just as I have loved you." The life of Jesus as a whole charts a distinctive way of loving that is normative for his disciples. In summary, "Jesus' way of acting and his words, his deeds and his precepts constitute the moral rule of Christian life" (20).

Jesus tells the young man that to seek God he must obey the commandments, specifically the second table of the Decalogue. The young man realizes that there could be more to life than following the commandments. He is so attracted by Jesus that he wants to take the next step, whatever it might be. Jesus invites him into the costly freedom of discipleship which carries morality to its perfection in love. "If you wish to be perfect, go, sell your possessions and give the money to the poor, then you will have treasure in heaven; then come, follow me" (Mt 19:21). The commandments are the indispensable first step on the road that leads to companionship with Jesus, but not the whole journey. The next step would mean leaving his wealth in order to join Jesus on the road that leads to the cross.

Although Jesus is held up as the norm for Christian moral life, the deontological way in which the encyclical applies biblical ethics sharply limits that normativity. His "way of acting, his words, [and] his deeds" do not appear to count as much as his precepts. Are they meant only to furnish examples of what the precepts are? The Pope's focus on the commandments most likely comes from his intention to demonstrate that the Church's magisterium can authoritatively teach universal moral prohibitions, a position which he believes has been challenged by some contemporary moral theologians. This hermeneutic restricts the contribution Scripture can make to the moral life. When you look at the gospels through the lens of deontology, what you discover, not surprisingly, are rules and principles. The dialogue with the Rich Young Man underwrites this deontological approach to ethics. It explicitly links the following of Christ to obeying the commandments. In fact, this passage is one of the few places in the Gospels where Jesus refers to the Decalogue.

Other lenses than deontology would allow one to see different aspects of Jesus' moral teaching. Liberation ethics and ethics of virtue pay more attention to the parables which challenge the usual moral presuppositions of his audience, to the healings and table-fellowship with the outcasts of his society which become paradigmatic for the compassion and justice which the disciples are to practice, and, finally, to the cross and resurrection which define the disciple's destiny. This fuller range of NT moral teaching indicates that Jesus charts the way of discipleship by doing more than establishing a teaching church which would reinforce universal moral standards. In the final chapter, I will argue that the key gospel text for applying the moral message of Jesus is "Go and do likewise" rather than "The one who hears you hears me."[22]

The difference between the advocates of faith ethics and the autonomy school on the use of Scripture stems from their contrasting modes of application. From their contrasting ethics flows a different selection of biblical materials. One side sees ethics primarily as a matter of rules and principles, the other as a more prudential evaluation based on competing values. Although their ethical naturalism leads them to select some of the same biblical material (prescriptive passages, appeals to human wisdom), they interpret these materials in distinctive ways which support different modes of application. Each school interprets Christology, for example, in ways that follow from and reinforce their preferred mode of application. The autonomy school prizes the incarnation as the ratification of human values which supports their confidence in an ethics of humane values. John Paul II emphasizes the cross, where Jesus preferred obedience to the Father's will over life itself and praises those who imitate him by making supreme sacrifices to obey "the inviolable holiness of God's law." (par 90)

The life of worship and preaching contributed to the excessive reliance upon law in the Catholic Church since the Council of Trent. The lectionary which prescribed the liturgical readings between Trent and the 1970's relied heavily on the Gospel of Matthew which stresses Jesus as teacher, clear moral prescriptions, and clear admonitions about the consequences of behavior leading to heaven and hell. John Mahoney points out that there is another vision of the moral life in the NT which attributes the unfolding of Christian moral life more to the sanctifying power of the Holy Spirit than the teaching power of the magisterium: "Such a non-Matthean approach is more in keeping with the Johannine and Pauline theologies of moral behaviour, with Christ and his Spirit as internal Teacher, and with the notion of conscience and subjectivity...."[23] As contemporary moral theology focuses more on the moral agent and less on the moral act, it is shifting its selection of biblical texts.

In the following chapters we will see that most theologians today concentrate on biblical teachings that refer to the agent rather than the moral act. Unlike the autonomy school, they are careful to show how Christian action flows from dispositions and perspectives that have been shaped by Scripture. Liberation theology makes a commitment to aid the poor and oppressed a necessary prerequisite for doing Christian theology or ethics. Stanley Hauerwas holds that the story of Jesus present in the Gospels and lived out in community governs the character of Christian agents by inculcating distinctive intentions and attitudes. In the final chapter I will argue that the analogical imagination links character with action that is consonant with Gospel values. All of these views are attempts to integrate the interior reality of "Christian intentionality" with distinctive ways of behavior that are both Christian and humane.

3
Call to Liberation

Liberation theologies, the most vital new voices in the latter part of the twentieth century, use Scripture to underwrite a commitment to the oppressed. They answer the moral question "What ought I to do?" with the most specific moral imperative we will see: "Act to liberate the oppressed because God is committed to them." Because God continues to act in history today as in biblical times, Scripture reveals the stance which Christians should take. Liberation theologies begin with a call to conversion which sets the hermeneutical agenda. They begin from a contemporary historical context as interpreted through social analysis and move to the biblical text to discover the attitudes which will inspire and sustain solidarity with the oppressed. Scripture does not dictate a political program or definite particular actions since the more concrete imperatives must emerge from attending to the oppressed and the specific structures that burden them.

There is no single "theology of liberation" because each one emerges from a specific social and economic context. The original theology of liberation came from Latin America in the pioneering work of Gustavo Gutierrez, a Peruvian Catholic. Analogous versions soon appeared in South Africa, Korea, the Philippines and other cultures; each analyzed their distinctive situation from a common theological starting point.[1] In the United States first black theologians such as James Cone and then feminist theologians adopted a similar point of departure but they had to approach the biblical text in different fashion because they were starting from different groups of oppressed peoples. Poverty and economic injustice are central concerns that run through the canon from Exodus to Revelation. Oppression based on race and gender, however, are not dominant biblical concerns. Not only that, Scripture becomes problematic as a moral resource for black or feminist theology when one recognizes that portions of it tolerate certain exploitative institutions like slavery and have been used for centuries to justify male domination and anti-Semitism. Since Scripture functions differently for theologians who are aligned with the poor than for those who begin from the experience of racial and gender oppression, we will treat them in distinct parts of this chapter. First we will examine the development of Gutierrez' work and the systematic reflections of Jon Sobrino who writes from El Salvador. Then we will focus on the writings of Elisabeth Schüssler Fiorenza who has set the terms of discussion in feminist hermeneutics of the New Testament.

Liberation theologians are usually more self-conscious about hermeneutics than those we have seen in the previous two models. The first hermeneutical challenge is the moral one that Scripture poses to its interpreters even before they open its cover. Interpreters must acknowledge their own "social location" and its inevitable limitations before they consider any portion of the Bible. Since every reading is a "situated reading," a high degree of honesty is required of the reader to acknowledge the multiple allegiances of class, gender, race, national position, educational status, etc. The challenge to be honest leads, it is hoped, to a new type of conversion which renounces the privileges of dominant status by joining in solidarity with the oppressed. Scripture reveals the true God only to those who read it from the standpoint of those to whom the word of God is primarily addressed, namely the oppressed. While the various liberation theologies agree that the suffering of the oppressed must be the starting point, they do not concur on which aspects of oppression are primary. Latin Americans have been faulted for ignoring the problems of patriarchy by first world feminists who have themselves been criticized for ignoring the oppressive effects of race and class by African Americans who articulate "womanist theology."[2] More recently, the interconnection of all forms of oppression and liberation is being noted.[3]

The second hermeneutical challenge facing liberation theology is the question of control. When a particular perspective controls the reading of the biblical text, will it allow Scripture to challenge its own presuppositions? Or will the Bible be reduced to providing rhetorical support for political agendas that have been derived on purely secular grounds? Obviously, liberation theology shares the problem of control with every other use of Scripture. No one is immune from the "hermeneutical circle," from "discovering" in Scripture interests that were in fact imported from prior assumptions. The hermeneutical circle can avoid vicious circularity if we allow Scripture to challenge the interests we bring to it. For example, the preferential option for the poor often comes from a faith perspective shaped by Scripture. Yet, not every attitude or strategy that might advance the cause of a particular group of oppressed people will be compatible with the witness of Jesus Christ. The pursuit of justice without forgiveness would run afoul of the Gospel. As Ignacio Gonzalez Faus expresses it, "One must fight a revolution as someone forgiven."[4] Every use of Scripture has to show that the Word of God remains a "two-edged sword" that can shape its presuppositions. Otherwise, the Word will be mere garnish to our unassailed preferences.

I. Advances in Latin American Liberation Theology

The call to liberation first sounded from Latin America following the Second Vatican Council and the meeting of the continent's Catholic bishops in 1968 in Medellín, Colombia. After centuries of being an intellectual colony of European theology, Latin America found its voice in a distinctive new approach. Perhaps it would be more accurate to say that liberation theology found its "voice" in the cry of the poor. This theology did not originate in the academy but from the historical event that Jon Sobrino describes as "the irruption of the poor on the social scene—their seeming sudden materialization as if from nowhere."[5]

"The irruption of the poor" was a historical event produced by a web of social forces; the poor broke into the consciousness of theology through history. Theology went from history to Scripture, not the other way around. Theologians did not discover "the cry of the poor" for a liberating Redeemer in Exodus but in the poor around them; then they went to Exodus and found the same Redeemer who had freed Israel. Gutierrez stresses the priority of history, which means the present socio-economic results of historical processes even more than the record of the past. He incorporates this priority into the structure of *A*

Theology of Liberation.[6] He begins from the specific history which makes the cry of the poor audible and enables the reader to take "the view from below."

A call to conversion stands at the outset of every liberation theology. Perhaps for the first time in Christian theology, theologians are required to live a form of political holiness. Theology is only a second act; the practice of liberation comes first. Many liberation theologians participate in basic Christian communities where the poor read Scripture to find meaning in their lives and inspiration in their struggle for justice. That popular urgency infiltrates their writings. If we stand with the privileged, how can we discover that the God of revelation is found on the side of the oppressed? Gutierrez writes that the times demand a militant reading of the Bible: "The Bible must be restored to the Christian peoples who believe and hope in the God who reveals himself there. Otherwise, all self-styled 'scientific' exegesis loses its validity."[7]

The term "option" in "preferential option for the poor" highlights the free commitment which is involved in this conversion. "It is a matter of deep, ongoing solidarity, a voluntary daily involvement with the world of the poor."[8] This pivotal choice constitutes the initial moral step and also the necessary epistemological standpoint, that is, the point at which genuine knowledge becomes possible. Since the poor are closer to the situation of the writers and the audiences of Scripture than those who are comfortable, the poor have an advantage in understanding Scripture's message.

The past quarter century has deepened and expanded the concerns of liberation theology, according to Sobrino.

Generally speaking, this is what we discovered in Latin America in the 1970's: that there could be no spiritual life without real life. We came to see that faith and justice, God and this oppressed world, Jesus and the poor, must be brought together—that, with historical and Christian urgency, a practice of liberation was needed. This being said, however, we also observed and saw that the practice of liberation could need to be imbued with spirit, and with a specific spirit, and this was the lesson of the 1980's that so many Christians—theologians among them—accepted with all their heart.[9]

The recent writings of Latin American liberationists testify to this development of method from a call to conversion to articulating the spirituality needed to sustain that commitment. We mentioned earlier that every adequate Christian ethics has four components: Scripture, tradition, a theory of what is normatively human (ethics), and empirical data relevant to the issues considered. The early work of Gutierrez, for example, emphasized the factual situation of Latin American oppression and a "utopian" view of a renewed humanity. In giving priority to these sources it resembled traditional Catholic moral theology. For moral theology natural law provided the vision of what is normatively human, where a specific form of historical and social analysis served that role in the early Gutierrez. His more recent writings are more exegetical in character and articulate a rich spirituality necessary to sustain the struggle for justice.

The Liberating Scripture

The *selection* of biblical materials has changed as liberation theology has developed. Gutierrez' early focus on Exodus and the prophets has not been lost, but broadened to include other material in the Old Testament which he interprets in a more Christological manner. "In Latin America today [1979], the spirituality of the exile is every bit as important as the Easter experience of resurrection. The joy of resurrection calls for many a death on a cross."[10] Deuteronomy stresses the contemporary claim of the covenant on all subsequent generations and reinforces a hermeneutics of present memory. Wisdom literature gives a more cosmological appreciation of the "God of life" and the psalms add a range of emotional responses to God.[11] Gutierrez has turned in the past few years to the Book of Job to ground a more contemplative approach to the profound problems raised by continuing injustice and human suffering. He protests in one of Scripture's most powerful passages that the sufferings of the poor are caused by the oppression of the rich, not by God (24:2–12). Job protests that he had taken the side of the poor, but to what point? "I was eyes for the blind, and feet for the lame. Who but me was a father to the poor?" (29:15–16) When God finally addresses him in his misery, Job comes to realize that

> justice alone does not have the final say about how we are to speak of God...the prophetic way is not the only way of drawing

near to the mystery of God, nor is it sufficient by itself…the issue
is not to discover gratuitousness and forget the duty of establishing what is right and just, but to situate the quest for justice in the
framework of God's gratuitous love.[12]

In his book *On Job*, Gutierrez places this work in his overall theological
framework of interpretation by linking Job's anguished discourse to the
cry of the slaves in Egypt and Jesus' cry of abandonment on the Cross.
The Exodus is the beginning of the story of God's response to the poor
while the Cross and Resurrection are its culmination.[13]

Gutierrez uses a wide range of New Testament material to demonstrate how pervasive is message that the Gospel is "good news for the
poor," the phrase from Isaiah 61:1 that Jesus cites at the outset of his
public ministry in Luke 4. The scene of the final judgment (Matt
25:31–46) has been a staple for showing that access to God comes
through practical solidarity with the poor. Increasingly, however,
Gutierrez has shifted attention to Matt 5: "The Beatitudes in Matthew
are therefore the Magna Carta of the congregation (the church) that is
made up of the disciples of Jesus."[14] In a dialectic of gift and demand,
promise and mission, they describe the ethics of the Reign of God
which Jesus inaugurates. The focus on concrete actions on behalf of the
poor "makes it possible to connect chapter 5 of Matthew, with which
the preaching begins, and chapter 25, with which this preaching
concludes… The proclamation of the kingdom begins with the promise
made to the poor in spirit and ends with the gift of the kingdom to those
who come to the aid of the materially poor."[15]

The Sermon on the Mount outlines the ethical requirements of
discipleship in stark antitheses in order to provoke the fundamental
choice between life and death, between the God of life and the idols that
bring death to the poor. This same disjunction runs through the
Johannine literature in its descriptions of light and darkness as well as
through the Pauline dichotomy between freedom and slavery.
Increasingly in Gutierrez' writing, Jesus becomes the focus of God's
liberating action in history. In his meditative *We Drink From Our Own
Wells*, Gutierrez draws heavily from the Gospel of Luke to show the
relation between Jesus and his disciples and then turns to Romans and
First Corinthians in particular to spell out the spirituality that makes it
possible to be disciples in the continuing community of faith.[16] While

Exodus was the theological center of gravity in his first work, Gutierrez' subsequent writings have relied far more on the New Testament to spell out the ethics of the Kingdom by examining the concrete ways of Jesus.

II. Interpreting the Ethics of Liberation

The exodus is not a self-interpreting event. Although the major liberation theologians have carefully set it in the context of themes about God, Jesus Christ and the Reign of God, some interpretations have been remarkably limited. Gilberto da Silva Gorgulho, for example, relies heavily on the materialist reading of Israel's origins proposed by Norman K. Gottwald.[17] Although the exodus and the distribution of the land are the central memory of a free Israel, the exodus turns out to be a religious myth borrowed to sanctify the taking of the land by the formerly dispossessed peoples of Canaan. Those who had experienced the exploitation of Pharaoh lent their memories to catalyze "this process of egalitarian, non-dominated social organization."[18] Yahweh's manifestation does not occur in the release from Egypt but at Sinai, where a new social and ethical awareness is expressed in the Decalogue and tribal laws. The paradigm for Israel's faith, therefore, becomes the self-wrought liberation of the land from oppressive masters. This reductionism shows the risk of "history reading history" as a hermeneutic. When a twentieth century materialist viewpoint edits out any transcendent dimension from the exodus event, one suspects that theology has been reduced to sociology with no remainder.

In Gutierrez the exodus is interpreted through theological themes that support a social strategy relevant to the Latin American situation.[19] He carefully connects, but does not identify, political liberation and God's liberation of us from sin. The Gospel does not provide us with concrete political strategies, but it does proclaim the Reign of God which is a vision that corresponds with God's promises. Gutierrez does not fall into the trap of the proponents of the social gospel in the early twentieth century who equated democratic reform with the arrival of God's Kingdom. When Walter Rauschenbusch wrote *Christianizing the Social Order*, he collapsed the two processes into a single development.[20]

The concept of liberation is a single process with three distinguishable levels of meaning for Gutierrez: "political liberation, human liberation throughout history, liberation from sin and admission to communion with God."[21] These levels are interdependent but cannot be reduced to a single dimension. The first level relies on scientific analysis of the structures of oppression and the commitment to transform them. This struggle has salvific significance because it attacks the structures of injustice that hinder the coming of the Kingdom. The second meaning of liberation depends on a vision of humanity that encourages people to take responsibility for their own destiny and inspires them with the hope of a just society. It is product of "utopian thinking," an ideal moral vision, and its projection into history. The third concept of liberation is not human achievement but the work of God, who liberates from sin. It operates on the level of faith rather than social analysis or utopian visions. These three processes work together: "Not only is the growth of the Kingdom not reduced to temporal progress; because of the Word accepted in faith, we see that the fundamental obstacle to the Kingdom, which is sin, is also the root of all misery and injustice; we see that the very meaning of the growth of the Kingdom is also the ultimate precondition for a just society and a new humanity."[22] Christ saved humanity from sin and all its consequences, including injustice and hatred. When Christians struggle against these same forces, they enter into the continuation of Christ's creative, salvific work.

Jesus the Liberator, the Reign of God, and the Poor

The three central theological symbols that interpret Scripture in Latin American liberation theology are Jesus Christ as Liberator, the Reign of God, and the poor to whom Jesus proclaimed it. In recent years, more systematic theological reflections have deepened the original insights and displaced most of the humanistic, neo-Marxist categories (class struggle, means of production, labor theory of value, utopia, etc.). Jon Sobrino has built on the work of Gutierrez. Latin Americans have access to the experience of Jesus because they can recognize an *analogy* between the message and fate of Jesus and the countless deaths they have witnessed; they do not rely on historical criticism alone. "These lives that today lead to this type of death have essentially the same structure as that claimed for the life of Jesus:

proclamation of the Kingdom to the poor, defence of the oppressed and confrontation with the oppressors, the proclamation of the God of life and the condemnation of idols."[23]

The death of Jesus was primarily a political execution motivated by the threat which his words and deeds engendered in the religious and secular establishments (A good number of first world theologians and exegetes have come to endorse this reading.) When Jesus attacked the systems that oppressed the poor and proclaimed that God was inaugurating a new Reign, he was also undermining the foundations of the oppressors' power and identity. All the groups that conspired together to kill him held some sort of power in Palestine. Their fears drove the accusations they levelled against him: political subversion, attacking the Temple, questioning Roman authority and taxation, and proclaiming himself a king. Sobrino points out the analogy that his interpretation rests upon: "the cross of Jesus points us to the crosses that exist today, but these in turn point to that of Jesus and are— historically—the great hermeneutic to enable us to understand why Jesus was killed...."[24] When people are martyred for pursuing justice, it cannot be dismissed as merely political because the death of Jesus was a political event. He proclaimed the Reign of God as a socio-political reality and those who killed him knew it. "The ultimate agent of Jesus' murder is that which Jesus disturbs: his society."[25]

This hermeneutic brings together the three central realities of the poor, the Reign of God and Jesus as Liberator. Each one illumines the other, particularly in the persecution and death of Jesus of Nazareth. What provoked such murderous opposition? The way of life which Jesus embodied, the Reign of God, stood in complete contradiction to the idolatrous system which is, in Sobrino's phrase, "the anti-Kingdom." His death was no mistake but the direct consequence of the life he lived. The anti-Kingdom killed Jesus in self-defense. This shows the Reign of God to be a conflictual reality since it repudiates the organized oppression which is the anti-Reign. The true God of life cannot co-exist with the idols of death and so they react in characteristic defense. In Latin America, the poor are precisely those who are in constant danger of death from the same idolatrous systems of exploitation and dominating power. Those who opt to stand with the poor in struggling for justice will soon experience the wrath of the anti-Reign.

The organizing theme of liberation links the three realities of Jesus, the Reign of God, and the poor. Theologians have identified the eschatological promise which is the center of Jesus' message with the Reign of God and the resurrection. The Reign of God was first proclaimed in a social situation which is remarkably similar to the reality of Latin America. By contrast, where theology has not discovered the poor, it has focused on the resurrection, which does not teach us how to live in history as effectively as does the Reign of God. Unfortunately, history testifies that concentrating on the final utopia of the resurrection "can and does feed an individualism without a people, a hope without a praxis, an enthusiasm without a following of Jesus—in sum, a transcendence without history."[26]

Although the Reign of God brings together transcendence and history, does it have any actual moral content? For this we need to turn to the gospel accounts of the life and ministry of Jesus which flesh out the promise. "What happens is that the global (the Kingdom of God) is expressed in the everyday, the details of Jesus' life, but these in turn are the expression of the global vision, of the Kingdom of God."[27] The healing miracles especially reveal that *mercy*, "the gripping of God's entrails at the sight of the suffering of the weak,"[28] is the primary and ultimate moral disposition of God's way of ruling. Mercy, therefore, is the central moral demand of Christian discipleship. Compassion takes its cues from the needs of those who are suffering. In the same way, the Reign of God becomes concrete by responding to those to whom it is proclaimed. Although Scripture assures us that God is love, "the addressee of the Reign makes that love concrete in terms of love for the weak, in terms of affection for the weak, and in terms of the defense of the weak."[29] Theology has too often taken a transcendent view of the sacrificial love of Jesus as fulfilling the will of the Father or making satisfaction rather than seeing his love as primarily the response of the God of life to those who are threatened by death in all its forms.

The option for the poor, therefore, defines and manifests God's grace. Poverty of itself does not make greater openness to God possible, nor is God obliged by the moral worth of the poor to act on their behalf. That act is completely gratuitous. Liberation theology does not seek to romanticize the poor or claim that they are the "spiritual proletariat" which is the vanguard of history, as Marx portrayed the urban proletariat. Jesus does not tell us why God is partial to the poor, simply that God is for them. That partiality gave constant scandal in his time and led to his death, but he never retreated from the claim that God's revelation is first of all "good news to the poor." There is no other reason for this divine option except that this is the way God is. Sobrino states that at this point we face the mystery of God, the unexplainable freedom that lies at the heart of God's gratuity.[30] While it is true that God wills the salvation of all, God begins with the poor and requires that the rest be converted to be in solidarity with the poor.

The Practice of Liberation

Liberation theology applies this biblical vision of the Kingdom to practice via a set of dispositions which guides critical discernment of particular socio-historical contexts. The strength of this approach is the motivational depth which it provides the disciple; its weakness is that it appears to leave the disciple without specific moral principles. The eschatological norm of the full Reign of God shapes liberation ethics as teleological, with a subordinate deontological dimension coming from the demand to identify with the poor because that is the will of God. God's call is unconditional because it leads to a death which defies human notions of personal fulfillment or effectiveness. Sobrino is skeptical of natural law ethics because it cannot grasp the paradox of the cross or the struggle for justice. Liberation theology does not accept natural law's basic principle, "Do good and avoid evil," because it should read instead, "Do good and eradicate evil and suffering from the world."

If traditional natural law could be characterized as an ethics in search of a theology, the work of Gutierrez and Sobrino has been criticized as a theology in search of an ethics.[31] It is developing a more articulate spirituality, but it is unclear that spirituality can do the work of ethics. Other liberationists have spelled out the philosophical basis of ethics more fully: the Argentinean Jose Miguez Bonino uses the criterion of "the maximizing of universal human possibilities and the minimizing of human costs" to concretize the option for the poor in questions of political and economic power.[32] Also, Enrique Dussel employs a theory of communal justice to apply to a range of social topics the absolute moral principle, "Liberate the poor."[33]

Scripture does not offer a fully developed philosophical ethics, and in this respect the liberationists probably reflect some of the limitations of the biblical text itself. As I shall argue in the final chapter, its appeal is more to the imagination of the Christian than to his or her powers of rational application of principles. The ethics in the writings of many liberationists is more analogical than abstractly logical. For instance, moving from the crucified peoples of today to the cross of Jesus and back offers illumination as it clarifies the religious meaning of suffering and confirms hope under persecution. It does not immediately provide prescriptions about what to do concretely. Insofar as moral reflection requires both prescription and illumination, the rich theological vision from Latin America needs to be developed through a more exact theory of justice.

Sobrino writes, "Today it is the concept of a just life that bridges the gap between the systematic and evangelical concept of the Reign."[34] However, he does not develop a theory of justice, perhaps because the outrageous unjust acts of oppressors are more obvious than the institutional policies which would make for justice in complex issues like land distribution. Without a theory of justice one cannot determine how certain moral standards should guide social transformation to prevent it from being corrupted by retribution and vindictive violence. We need some clarity about what is normatively human in order to develop a theory of justice: What are the inalienable rights, even of one's enemies? What guarantees can be cited for the protection of human dignity and equality in the new society? (Admittedly, these questions are framed in first-world, post-Enlightenment terms, but they are not superfluous to Latin American struggles.) A philosopher might criticize a liberation ethics of dispositions and discernment by paraphrasing Immanuel Kant, "Principles without dispositions are lifeless, but dispositions without principles are blind."

At the present stage in liberation theology the gap between vision and action is bridged by a *spirituality and the practice of discernment*. The spirituality is a set of dispositions based on the example of Jesus and the needs of the poor that enables "life lived in the spirit of Jesus," in Sobrino's phrase.[35] The fundamental disposition is love which must be expressed in mercy. This is prior even to the normative set of Christian dispositions expressed in the Beatitudes, to which Sobrino and Gutierrez turn to ground morality. The Beatitudes are the promise of the Reign of God to the poor and persecuted, but also the profile of Jesus and the disciple. The Spirit enables the community to discern how that profile should be adapted to its circumstances: "Jesus should be followed, continued, updated in history—not imitated," cautions Sobrino.[36] In a dialectical movement, the Spirit adapts Jesus to a specific time and place and yet always leads the disciple back to the same profile of Jesus of Nazareth. Among his traits are partiality toward the poor, fortitude, creativity, joy, and gratuity. These traits are not simply deduced from Scripture but learned from the poor as one joins their struggles and has the experiences of solidarity that can disclose the true meaning of the Bible. As these dispositions take root in disciples, they should have a sharper sense of what actions and strategies are appropriate. That is, they should be able to discern whether these actions correspond to the central realities of faith or fail to do so. This discernment presumes the capacity for prayerful evaluation to sort out the options which practical reflection has derived from the historical situation of action.

A profound contemplative dimension also is coming to the fore in recent Latin American writings. The long struggle against oppression has led many deeper into the obscure yet gracious mystery of God in a way that animates active praxis for justice. Since the murder of his fellow Jesuits in San Salvador in 1989, Sobrino has begun to write in a more narrative fashion about these martyrs and especially the assassinated Archbishop Romero as exemplars of the way of Jesus. Thomas Schubeck writes that Gutierrez' "lifelong commitment to the poor enabled him to discover how Job's awareness of solidarity with those suffering unjustly led Job to discover God's gratuitous love in silent contemplation. Job came to recognize that he did not understand everything about social justice and so needed to hear God's word at a more profound level."[37] Sobrino describes the dynamic of practice and contemplation: "We encounter God in bringing the divine goodness to a concrete realization, which is practice, and in letting God be God, which is contemplation. We encounter God in responding to a God of complete otherness and in corresponding to God by rendering the divine reality itself real in our history."[38]

III. Feminist Hermeneutics and Liberation

Liberation theology can no longer be considered a single voice. In the past decade it has become a polyphonic, if not always harmonious, chorus. When different marginated groups find their theological voice, they also interpret Scripture in distinctive ways. The canonical text becomes more problematic in these other expressions than it is for most Latin American theologians. While Scripture takes a relatively consistent stand against the oppression of the poor, it says little about patriarchy, racism, or imperialism. Even worse, Scripture has been used to reinforce practices and institutions of oppression. Nevertheless, every Christian theologian coming from these different marginated groups wrestles with Scripture. The very argument testifies to the centrality of Scripture in forming Christian identity; those who dismiss it almost always end up in a post-Christian stance.

It is impossible to treat here all the various theologies of liberation that have emerged. I will focus on the one which has debated the hermeneutical questions most fully, namely North American feminism. Mary Ann Tolbert distinguishes three uses of Scripture by "reformist" feminists (that is, those who intend to remain within Christianity): a) focusing on the prophetic-liberation tradition within the canon as the test of other material; b) "the remnant standpoint" which retrieves texts concerning women that have been distorted or ignored by patriarchal hermeneutics; and c) "the shift from text to history" which "eschews the present canon almost entirely and turns instead to the reconstruction of biblical history."[39] We will examine the writing of Elisabeth Schüssler Fiorenza, who pioneered the third alternative but at times also utilizes the second. She studied in Germany but has taught in the United States for the past twenty years. Her work raises hermeneutical and moral questions about the use of Scripture in contemporary discussions of liberation.

The Original Discipleship of Equals

Since her 1984 work *In Memory of Her: A Feminist Theological Reconstruction of Christian Origins* Schüssler Fiorenza has pursued two parallel projects.[40] The first is a feminist hermeneutic that seeks to reclaim the biblical heritage for the emancipation of woman. The second project is *historiographical* since it attempts to reconstruct the historical origins of Christianity through clues in the biblical text which indicate that the early Christian movement was a community of radical equality which quickly was suppressed by patriarchal, hierarchical patterns of church organization. The New Testament witnesses to this community of equals indirectly. "Biblical texts about women therefore are like the tip of an iceberg, intimating what is submerged and obliterated in historical silence. They have to be read as touchstones of the historical reality that they both repress and construct." These texts have to be extracted from the canon and reassembled "like mosaic stones in a feminist design which, rather than recuperating the marginalizing or oppressive tendencies of the text, is able to counteract it."[41] She does not present this early community as an objective fact but as "a plausible 'subtext' to the androcentric text."[42] The design of the new mosaic is provided by her central critical principle which is the experience of women's struggle against oppression. Commitment to that project serves the same role that the preferential option for the poor does for Latin American liberationists. It requires a basic conversion of attitudes: women must not only shed the counter-identity imposed upon them by Western gender stereotypes but also the self-effacement and alienation which they cause.

Schüssler Fiorenza's *hermeneutical* project is connected to the historiographical one by this common starting point and a common method, namely rhetorical analysis. It works from the premise that all texts express the interests of their authors and are designed to reinforce the perspectives of particular groups in power. The texts of the dominant group, however, do not succeed in completely silencing the rest of humanity, since they can be heard through the contradictions, silences, and repressive strategies evident in the establishment texts. Contemporary readers must resolutely apply a "hermeneutics of suspicion" (Paul Ricouer's phrase) to unmask the repressive strategies in the canonical text.[43] When the excluded voices are noticed and brought to the center, the Bible can cease to play a repressive role and begin to become emancipatory.

The New Testament should be read as a conflict between two rhetorical traditions. On the one side are texts on the leadership of women, clues about the inclusive structure of early communities, the principle of radical equality in Gal 3:28, etc. On the other side are the patriarchal rhetoric of Paul, the sanitized version of Christian beginnings in Luke-Acts, and the household codes in Ephesians, Colossians, and the Pastoral Epistles which reinforce cultural roles of domination and submission. One must give full attention to the oppressive interests of the gospel writers when reading texts about women. Schüssler Fiorenza derives the title of her latest book, *But She Said*, from the story of the Syro-Phoenician woman in Mark 7:24–30. When analyzed rhetorically, it becomes a paradigm for feminist practice: "The woman, characterized ethnically and culturally as a religious outsider, enters the theological argument, turns it against itself, overcomes Jesus' prejudice, and achieves the well-being of her little daughter. As distinct from all other controversy stories, Jesus does not have the last word."[44]

What or who exercises moral authority in this critical feminist ethics? Not the text itself, since it so often reinforces oppression. Nor any portion of the text, nor a "canon within the canon" like positive passages on women, nor the prophetic tradition, because it still uses words of men to define the reality of women. The canon as whole cannot balance out the patriarchal, oppressive sections within it because if they are taken to be the word of God, then the God it proclaims is oppressive and dehumanizing. No single ordering principle or doctrine, including the exodus or liberation, can be authoritative since that would reduce the rich diversity of Scripture to an abstract essence. Neither can Jesus be the normative principle. Schussler Fiorenza criticizes Sobrino for holding that following the historical Jesus gives us access to the Christ of faith because we cannot know the historical Jesus.[45] In addition, it is actually harmful for women. "Focusing on the figure of Jesus, the Son of the Father, when reading the Bible, 'doubles' women's oppression. Women in the act of reading not only suffer from the alienating division of self against self but also from the realization that to be female is to be neither 'divine' nor 'a son of God.'"[46] The normative principle for reading Scripture cannot be derived from the text itself but only from women's experience of struggling against oppression. A critical feminist hermeneutics must assess the Bible with one aim in view: "whether and how Scripture can become an enabling, motivating resource and empowering authority in women's struggle for justice, liberation, and solidarity."[47]

From History to Praxis

The moral material of Scripture cannot be applied directly to contemporary issues. Instead, Scripture should be used as a "formative root metaphor" of feminist practice, as a *flexible prototype* rather than a *timeless archetype* which dictates perennial patterns of belief and behavior. When read as a "formative root-model," Scripture is understood as "an open-ended paradigm that sets experience in motion and makes transformation possible."[48] Scripture is not the foundation document of the community nor does it offer a set of moral principles to shape Christian identity. "Rather, as the formative prototype of biblical faith and community, the Scriptures offer paradigms of struggles and visions that are open to their own transformations through the power of the Spirit in ever new socio-historical locations."[49] Today this development occurs through a highly sophisticated critical hermeneutics and rhetorical analysis and also through imaginative poetic expressions of oppressed women. Genuine inspiration comes when a community wrestles with the text in light of its own problems. Here, the inspired community is "the church of women" (which remains rather vague but seems to include all who struggle for liberation, believers and nonbelievers).

Like Sobrino and Gutierrez, Schüssler Fiorenza advocates a spirituality to sustain the struggle and to envision a different reality from the oppressive past and present. Although hers is not as spelled out as theirs, it is supposed to do the work of ethics by bridging conviction and practice. The content of her spirituality, however, does not come from Jesus of Nazareth or Scripture. It comes from "the logic of democracy" which "requires passionate involvement, respect, and recognition of the other, desire for justice, recognition of needs, zest for life, the capacity to relate to others, and especially the vision of a different community of equals."[50] She describes this spirituality of vision as "incarnational theology," which stresses "the mutual indwelling of G-d and of G-d in the world; the saving collaboration between Christ and the believer; and the Spirit of G-d, Divine Wisdom, as a living fountain, a 'festal dance of blazing love.'"[51] This trinitarian expression is a rare instance in which Schüssler Fiorenza alludes to the religious symbols of her Catholic tradition. She employs the term "G-d" in more recent work to express her reluctance to speak of the divinity in positive terms, since God belongs "in the realm of the ineffable."[52] Although these religious symbols are invoked, they do not appear to affect materially the democratic ideals which give content to Schüssler Fiorenza's spirituality. The profile of the original community of radical equality and the dispositions recommended in her spirituality are derived from contemporary democratic ideals that stand on their own apart from any religious framework. Often they appear to be retrojected back into the consciousness of first century communities.

One wonders whether there is much of Scripture left for Christian ethics in this approach. In fairness to her stated project, Schüssler Fiorenza disavows any intention of proposing a complete Christian ethics or constructing a systematic theology. She writes as a historical critic and an interpreter of Christian origins whose work will be incorporated into Christian ethics by others. Some have doubts whether the little that survives her criticism will be of much use to ethics. Tolbert questions whether "*any* historical reconstruction can form the basis of Christian faith and practice."[53] Just as the quest for the historical Jesus failed to get behind the New Testament to a more primitive historical reality, the quest for reconstructing an early community of radical equality has severe limits. Schüssler Fiorenza's program seems to be primarily criticism and unmasking of the androcentric interests that shaped the biblical text and Christian tradition. The emancipatory praxis she recommends consists mostly of discourse rather than action: new discursive communities who spell out alternative philosophies, visions and stories for women. Or perhaps the discourse *is* emancipatory action.

Sobrino and Gutierrez have been faulted for defining the Reign of God too directly from their identification with the needs of the Latin American poor. It could be that Schüssler Fiorenza's social location in the secular American university has had the opposite effect. While they learn from the piety and gospel hope of the poor, her interlocutors appear to be a small group of highly educated scholars in the secular academy. This social location seems to dictate an approach that is morally committed but religiously impoverished. Its thoroughgoing "hermeneutics of suspicion" nullifies any challenge that the canonical text might make back on the feminist interpreter. Sobrino has frankly acknowledged that the struggle for liberation in Latin America has led to temptations and moral pitfalls which conflict with the gospel vision of the Reign of God.[54] When that vision is reduced to a general mandate to struggle against oppression, it loses any capacity to challenge Schüssler Fiorenza's position. Anthony Thiselton raises the key problem for any advocacy theology: "Why should 'our' community experience *as such* claim any critical status as over against that of others? The potentially transforming effect of engagement with the 'other' not least through biblical texts is to de-centre our pre-occupation with our own criteria of relevance by enlarging our horizons to embrace a wider understanding."[55] The Word of God acts as a two-edged sword when it cuts through our own biases, not only those of our opponents.

The end result of Schüssler Fiorenza's complex project is a moral argument that seems minimally religious. An unknowable divinity indirectly supports movements of emancipation but does not act in history except through the feminine principle of Sophia which is mentioned in OT Wisdom literature but has no concrete historical manifestation. Revelation occurs in women coming to consciousness rather than in divine self-disclosure. Biblical images, once purged of their androcentric traits, have rhetorical and pragmatic value for the struggle, but they do not reveal anything true about the divine. The eschatological thrust of Scripture is missing because the divinity does not promise or effect the coming of the *basileia*. It seems to me that a Christianity without Jesus of Nazareth is as empty as Judaism would be without Moses or Abraham. The exodus and the cross and resurrection are ruled out as normative for the life of faith because Moses and Jesus are male.

The contrast between the spiritualities of the Latin Americans and the secular ideals endorsed by Schüssler Fiorenza is rather stark. The centrality of mercy even toward one's enemies, the rich hope forged in suffering, the grounding of obligation in gratitude, the paradox of waging revolution as one forgiven, the solidarity with the victim that extends even to martyrdom are all grounded in contemplation of Scripture by people who believe that it discloses how God deals with the world. The problem may lie with Schüssler Fiorenza's method itself. One wonders whether it takes into account the full experience of Christian and Jewish women. Perhaps the poor women of Latin American have a more vital spirituality rooted in the biblical tradition than women of the first world.[56] Or perhaps the experience of first world women who do have a developed Christian spirituality has not been counted as valid "women's experience."

Other American feminists have taken a different approach to the problematic canon of Scripture. They have turned to a source of moral theology which Schüssler Fiorenza discounts, namely *tradition* as the ongoing reflection of the entire believing community on Scripture and experience under the guidance of the Spirit. Lisa Sowle Cahill states that this is the most authoritative of the four sources of moral theology.

Relying on the work of Phyllis Trible, she appeals to the Genesis accounts of the creation of woman and man to ground a Christian sexual ethic of equality and mutuality. Even if the authors of Genesis did not intend to endorse these values, the literary expression points in their direction. Over time, the believing community came to realize the "trajectory" of these foundational texts and appreciate their moral potential which had been obscured in more patriarchal cultures.[57]

Sandra M. Schneiders objects to Schüssler Fiorenza's proposal that the offensive portions of the canon should be denied revelatory status. The analogy of the Declaration of Independence shows how the interaction between the foundational text of a community and those who continue to interpret it over time can free the text from the limitations of its original authors.

> The fact is that the believing community, like the American people in relation to the nation's founding documents, has grown and developed on the basis of its founding documents beyond the narrow perspective of the original articulators of the Christian vision.... From the gospel, Christians have learned that women for whom Jesus died are not inferior to men for whom he died, and that when Jesus condemned the attempt of his followers to lord it over one another he was also condemning the patriarchalism that is the foundation of sexism, clericalism, colonialism, classism, and all other forms of domination that have marred the Christian tradition.[58]

Texts which are oppressive to a particular group at a specific time might become an important resource for persons in other situations. If we discount the authority of Scripture because of its authors' biases or the subsequent uses to which it has been put, we might be rejecting the very resource which can transform the present. Minimally, the liberating sections of the biblical text can be cited against the oppressive sections. More importantly, the ongoing tradition of the community of faith offers a continuing corrective because subsequent readings of Scripture create "reservoirs of meaning" which enable it to be a living word for today. However, that development requires the social location of a faithful community rather than the secular academy or purely political movements.

Liberation theology insists on action in solidarity with the oppressed as the fulcrum for changing the moral agent. Even though it does not claim the competence to prescribe the practical remedies of injustice, it highlights the attitudes necessary for social transformation. The next two chapters focus more on the transformation of the moral agent and the believing community. How do the symbols and perspectives of Scripture take root in the Christian? How does the person change so that the proverbial heart of stone becomes a perceptive and responsive heart of flesh? Both the new moral theology and liberation thought moved from the human situation to Scripture. The next chapters will show how insights gained from biblical perspectives illumine and redefine the human situation. Can Scripture shape a distinctively Christian viewpoint that will penetrate moral problems to reveal and enable a faithful response?

4
Call to Discipleship

In the final two models we turn more to the moral agent and high-light the use of Scripture in transforming the "moral psychology," that is, the habits, dispositions, and identity which lead to a distinctively Christian way of acting. The social location moves from the struggle for liberation to the believing community whose common life transforms the believer. In this chapter, the identity or character of the agent is the focus, while the model of the next chapter concentrates on the deeper emotions and moral dispositions of the agent. These models bring Jesus of Nazareth more to the center of concern for ethics because disciples pattern their lives on their master. Christian discipleship approaches the moral life with the conviction that the most appropriate path is the one already blazed by Jesus and that the Christian must creatively embody that way of life in all situations. The moral question, "What ought I to do?" is recast in more particular terms: "How should I act as a disciple of Jesus in these circumstances?" The answer is found through a process of discernment which imaginatively seeks a way that responds to the continuous invitation to follow Jesus. The call to discipleship continues within the experience of the committed believer particularly through the assembly of faith called the Church.

A disciple is literally someone who learns from a master or guide, one who voluntarily enters a form of spiritual apprenticeship with a person he or she greatly respects. Discipleship implies a training that gradually incorporates the master's wisdom and example into the disciple's life. As these values and convictions deepen, she or he will move toward a more mature and creative fidelity which goes beyond externally copying the master's ways. The behavior of the mature disciple will emerge from convictions and habits which have become part of the person's character. Where Barth and Bonhoeffer stressed the command of God being addressed to the believer at discrete moments, the ethics of discipleship relies more on the abiding continuities of conviction and virtue which shape a person's steady identity over time. If the focus of deontology is *doing*, the virtue ethics behind discipleship stresses *being* and *becoming*. The mode of becoming especially suits discipleship, which connotes a gradual process of unlearning the ways of the world and taking on the way of Jesus. Actions flow from maturing dispositions like compassion and justice rather than from external commands. The New Testament does not indicate that people will often receive direct commands from God but rather that God inspires individuals and communities through steady, less dramatic means.

The NT has many passages which speak of the conversion and training of discipleship, the gradual assimilation of the person to the "mind of Christ." In the final discourse in John's gospel Jesus promises, "When he comes, the Spirit of truth, he will guide you to all truth" (Jn 16:13). When Paul moves from his great doctrinal vision in Romans to the section which applies it, he calls his audience to a conversion that will lead to moral wisdom: "I urge you therefore...to offer your bodies as a living sacrifice, holy and pleasing to God, your spiritual worship. Do not conform yourself to this age but be transformed by the renewal of your mind, that you may discern what is the will of God, what is good and pleasing and perfect" (Rom 12:1–2). The Letter to the Ephesians exhorts Christians to "live a life worthy of the calling you have received, with perfect humility, meekness, and patience, bearing with one another lovingly" (Eph 4:1–2). The authors presume that the initial conversion to God in Christ will become a continuing factor in moral experience. The call becomes a calling when it functions as an internal sounding board to help discern which actions correspond to the way of Jesus. It will not work like a moral compass which anyone can read, but more like a tuning fork which helps someone with a well trained ear to bring a piano into tune. The community of faith is the place where this training gradually takes place through personal example and practices of worship, service, reconciliation, and mutual support.

In this chapter we will focus on *narrative* and *parable* which are the two forms of biblical literature that have received the most attention in the past two decades. Stanley Hauerwas pioneered "narrative theology" which focuses on the distinctive story of Jesus as the pattern of Christian character and the collective identity of the Christian community. John R. Donahue and a number of other exegetes turn to the NT parables to discover "the gospel in cameo," pithy stories that capture the dynamics of the fuller story of Jesus and the Reign of God.[1] Through analyzing narrative and parable, they show how Scripture challenges the reader's deepest identity and presuppositions in order to shape "a life worthy of the calling you have received." These theologians concentrate on the particular words and actions of Jesus as God's revelation of a distinctive way of life for believers to follow. They do not reduce Jesus to a sage who dispenses moral wisdom to his followers, nor do they make him the content of his message. He announced the beginning of the reign of God and brought about reconciliation with God through his life, death, and resurrection. Even though he proclaimed a message of salvation rather than morality, the gospel story and parables provide a wealth of details that make him an example to follow, an engaging model for believers to learn from.

I. Narrative Theology and A Community of Character

Stanley Hauerwas selects biblical narratives as the most important literature for Christian ethics. He interprets these stories through a distinctive ecclesiology which emphasizes that the Church should be a "community of character" which shapes its members to stand against the dominant liberal culture of secular society. Jesus' prophetic mission should challenge the individualism and violence of contemporary American culture and build an alternative culture of faithful disciples. In his earlier writings he applied the biblical narrative through an ethics of character in which the virtues embedded in the story of Jesus are embodied in Christian vision and character.[2] In more recent work he has written less about character and more about the Church. From the social location of American Methodism he articulates a cultural critique which examines practices and institutions in light of religious convictions.[3]

The narratives of Mark are a favorite moral resource for Hauerwas because it starkly contrasts the way of the Kingdom and that of the world. The would-be disciples are confused by false notions of who the Messiah should be and what he will do. The Gospel of Mark centers on the collision between Peter's understanding of the messianic program and that of Jesus. In doing so, it shows how story defines discipleship. In Mk 8:27—9:1, Peter first acknowledges that Jesus is the Christ and then immediately rejects Jesus' description of the way of suffering and death that lies ahead. "Jesus thus rebukes Peter," writes Hauerwas, "who had learned the name but not the story that determines the meaning of the name."[4] In Peter's script, "the Christ" was supposed to be the victorious Messiah who would restore the power and glory of Israel. Jesus spells out a different scenario which must be embraced by his disciples. "If anyone would come after me let him deny himself and take up his cross and follow me. For whoever would save his life will lose it; and whoever loses his life for my sake and the Gospel's will save it. For what does it profit anyone to gain the whole world and forfeit his life?" (Mk 8:34–36) This scandalous story challenges Peter's very identity and exposes the falsity of his ambitions. Either this story changes Peter and the other hearers so that they embark on that fateful journey or else they cease to be Jesus' disciples.

Mark's Gospel highlights the temptation narratives to demonstrate how different the way of Jesus is from the customary ways of the world. "Mark's narrative artistry surfaces when we see that only by following Jesus' way to the cross can his disciples come to recognize his true character as the Son of God."[5] This gospel stresses renunciation (8:34) and humility expressed in service (10:42–45) over the temptation to riches and domination. It ends with the centurion recognizing that the broken man on the cross is truly the Son of God (15:39). Mark's gospel manifests the central ethical motif of the Old Testament: God is to be imitated by God's people. Remembering means letting our actions be determined by God's way of doing things, as Deuteronomy states it: "So you too must befriend the alien, for you were once aliens yourselves in the land of Egypt" (Dt 10:19). We have come to know God's holiness by God's faithfulness toward us; the story of that fidelity then sets the pattern for our actions.

Matthew's Sermon on the Mount mandates this imitation of God when it commands us to be perfect as God is perfect by indiscriminate loving, even of our enemies (Matt 5:43–48). The Sermon with all its demanding sayings does not set an impossible ideal unless we abstract it from the life of Jesus and the community that follows him. "The Sermon is but the form of his life, and his life is the prism through which the Sermon is refracted." However, we inevitably misinterpret it if we read it apart from the community of faith because "it is a description of the virtues of a community that embodies the peace that Christ has made possible among those who have been baptized into his cross and resurrection."⁶ The Beatitudes are not a list of virtues addressed to the solitary believer; they presume a social reality where people exist in new sorts of relations that exemplify and foster these qualities. The hard sayings of the Sermon on the Mount about living simply, chastely, nonviolently, etc., "are designed to remind us that we cannot live without depending on the support and trust of others."⁷ These demands are unintelligible unless they are read from a community which already practices nonviolence and reconciliation.

The way of the Reign of God is the path that the story of Jesus graphically displays. It cannot be resolved into a general teaching on self-sacrifice or an abstract ethical lesson on the trials of living virtuously. The message is inseparable from the person of Jesus. We cannot learn the truth of God's Reign without following the way of Jesus; his story defines God's way of ruling, which is paradoxically bound to the defeat of the cross. As Origen put it, Jesus is the *autobasileia*: God's reign incarnate. "Indeed the very announcement of the reality of the Kingdom, its presence here and now, is embodied in his life…. In him we see that living a life of forgiveness and peace is not an impossible ideal but an opportunity now present. Thus Jesus' life is integral to the meaning, content and possibility of the kingdom."⁸ Is it possible for anyone else to take this path? It becomes possible in the confidence that we are invited into the reign of God which has become a reality in Jesus' life and work.

Story and Church Form Christian Identity

It is no accident that Hauerwas returns frequently to the pivotal question of Jesus in Mark 8:29: "Who do you say that I am?" The central question of ethics for him is "Who do you say that you are?" The question of identity, self-understanding, is the key to interpreting Scripture and applying it in the moral life. Personal identity comes through a process of identification with a larger narrative framework—a story—and with a community that tries to live out that story—the Church. Hauerwas draws on the work of philosopher Alasdair MacIntyre to assert that every ethics depends upon the narrative of some community. Although contemporary culture pretends to transcend tradition and a formative narrative, it has one nonetheless. The great unacknowledged story of liberal democracy depicts the autonomous agent who lives according to self-interest, enters only contractual relationships, and values a maximum range of freedom above all. The universalist ethics which is widely endorsed by philosophers today is deceptive because it ignores the situated, contextual character of morality.[9] Ethics cannot be universalist, that is, applicable to every rational person in the same way, because ethics always depends on some specific account of human flourishing which is conveyed through a specific tradition.

Identity, story, and church are so interrelated in Hauerwas' ethics that it is difficult to mention one without the other. What we do and how we do it are ultimately rooted in a way of life, which is recounted in a story that shapes our self-understanding and that of the communities to which we belong. No one can have a completely private story since a way of life is always determined by a specific community to which we are loyal. We learn how to be virtuous by the example of others in the community when their witness inspires us to be virtuous. The common story shapes a community capable of ordering a way of life appropriate to this story. Every way of life has its own story; what is distinctive about Christians' community, the Church, is the story of Jesus of Nazareth.

Let us begin with the connection between *story and personal identity*.[10] For Hauerwas, Christian ethics aims to transform the self-understanding of the agent. Individuals are not only fragmented but they are deceived by the Enlightenment story which portrays the self as autonomous and not inherently dependent upon others. This dominant story which shapes the character of the would-be disciple clashes with the story of Jesus. The costly sayings of the gospels disturb us because they assault our complacent self-understanding, which would like the Gospel to co-exist peacefully with the ways of the dominant culture.

Hauerwas makes the *Church* central to the interpretation of Scripture. The Church not only proclaims the story of Jesus, but it must embody that narrative in its practices and relationships. We begin to read Scripture correctly when we start from the actual social reality of a church, not from any theory or specific doctrine. Hauerwas roundly criticizes literary hermeneutics which presume that the act of interpretation happens when an isolated reader engages a text. Private reading of Scripture has been the bane of American Christianity since it divorces the reader from the community of faith and encourages arbitrary, subjective interpretation. The Bible then becomes "America's book" because it confirms the unexamined nationalism of the reader. Historical criticism fosters this abuse of the doctrine of *sola Scriptura* as much as does fundamentalism because they share a common assumption: "By privileging the individual interpreter, who is thought capable of discerning the meaning of the text apart from the considera-tion of the good ends of a community, fundamentalists and biblical critics make the Church incidental."[11] The truth of the text cannot be known unless the reader has begun to be transformed, which can only happen by being initiated into a community that teaches new ways of living.

The Church is a *community of character* in a double sense because it both has a corporate character composed of its own self-understanding, practices, and rituals and it forms the characters of its members by proclamation and example. It serves as a school of God's Reign by fostering specific practices where we become capable of what seemed impossible: "forgiveness of enemies even unto death, loving service knowing no boundaries or limits, trust in the surpassing power of God's peace. In short, God has invited us to learn the skills, disciplines, and necessities of his kingdom...."[12] The Church does not have a social ethics so much as it *is* a social ethics by offering the world an alternative place to live. The eschatological reality of the Reign of God is breaking in through the social body of the Church, even though we cannot identify the two realities. Christian ethics, therefore, must be done from the Church in the form of a continuous critique of secular culture precisely at those points where Christians are tempted to collapse the tension between God's reign and the world. "Without the kingdom ideal, the church loses its identity-forming hope; without the church, the kingdom ideal loses its concrete character."[13]

Hauerwas and other narrative theologians have spelled out the implications of this conversion more thoroughly than most liberation theologians. They insist that the process of conversion must go beyond opting for the oppressed and entering their struggle, because the worldly habits of Christians must be transformed or else the option for the oppressed could result in a politics of resentment and vengeance. Stephen E. Fowl and L. Gregory Jones write that Scripture does not simply create a new world by being proclaimed. The emphasis should be placed, rather, on developing the skills needed to live in that new world. This re-education calls for a continuous diagnosis of what is wrong with the old way of life. "Such learning is a lifelong process requiring as a necessary correlative, at least in most social settings, a rather extensive unlearning of believers' old habits, dispositions, and judgements."[14]

None of these authors claim to have found an ideal Church community, but they represent a significant movement in mainstream American Protestantism. Hauerwas is a Southern Methodist, Fowl an Anglican, and Jones a United Methodist. They write from the social location of American Protestant churches whose numbers and influence have diminished steadily in American culture since the middle of the century. A liberal social agenda combined with a therapeutic individualism seemed to take the place of doctrinal clarity about Jesus Christ and the message of the Gospel. If they were writing in the third world, they would probably have a greater sense of urgency about oppression; for the United States, violence and nationalism may be more pertinent threats. A Roman Catholic observer is surprised to hear American Protestant theologians attacking private interpretation of Scripture, supporting ecclesial authority in doctrine and morals, calling for the witness of saints as exemplars of Christian holiness, and stressing the Eucharistic celebration as the central act of the Church's identity. These theologians do not want to become Catholics; rather, they are recovering features of a common heritage forgotten by churches which, in their view, had become more closely identified with the American dream than the Gospel.

Applying the Story

Hauerwas has addressed a wide range of moral issues in the past twenty years: marriage and divorce, abortion and the place of children, the disabled and mentally retarded, rational suicide and termination of life, medical experimentation on children, the nuclear question and pacifism, possessions and American consumerism, etc. Scripture enters into these discussions as the theological horizon against which current practices are analyzed. It rarely provides a "solution" because ethics for Hauerwas is less a question of *what* to do than *how* to do what we do. Since the medium of scholarly prose is no substitute for the reflections of a faithful believing community, he is not obliged to prescribe solutions in a professorial manner. Typically, Hauerwas writes as a cultural critic by holding up a problematic institution or practice and shows how the assumptions of post-Enlightenment individualism feed the confusion. The dominant ethics muddles the issue by appealing to the rights of individuals based on their abstract personhood and ignores their context and specific relations. He then proposes looking at the people affected through a biblically informed appreciation of how they are related to God and the rest of us are related to them.

For instance, he argues that the medical profession needs the Church because it is called to practice compassionate presence to those in pain. "Christians, drawing on the life of Jesus, tend to make the very pointlessness of suffering morally significant.... The cross provides a pattern of interpretation which allows one to locate the pointlessness of suffering within a cosmic framework."[15] Hauerwas draws on the psalms and the story of Job's comforters to uncover a general human obligation which is obscured when other frameworks are used. Physicians often interpret suffering through a mechanical model which sees it as a systemic breakdown. Consequently, they are liable to miss their basic obligation which is not to cure every malady, but "to care through being present to the one in pain."[16] Presumably, Christians caring for the sick can bring out this truth even to medical professionals who are not believers.

The question of violence and war is for Hauerwas the clearest line of demarcation between the world and the Church. Christians are people who can take the risk of forgiving in a world of violence and injustice. "They are able to break the circle of violence as they refuse to become part of those institutions of fear that promise safety by the destruction of others."[17] The national state is the main institution which defends itself through the threat of violence. Those who believe that liberal democracy is either a necessary defense for the Church or the beginning of the Reign of God on earth are deluded. "For democracy has in fact become an end in itself that captures our souls in subtle ways that we hardly notice. We thus stand ready to kill in order to preserve America against her enemies—enemies who are necessarily defined as totalitarian and thus anti-Christian."[18] The Jesus of the gospels is nonviolent and preaches detachment from possessions, which we are tempted to defend even by violence. In order to become a nonviolent Church, American Christians would have to willingly dispossess themselves of this attachment to what they own. Increasingly, Hauerwas turns to the ritual of the eucharistic banquet to show that violence makes no sense for Christians. "For it is in that meal, that set of habits and relations, that the world is offered an alternative to the habits of disunity which war breeds."[19] The table of the Lord treats strangers as welcome guests rather than threats to the community's particular identity, which is the usual motivation for excluding strangers.

Narrative ethics may fall under the rubric of an ethics of character and virtue, but including it in the context of community opens a significant role for rules and principles. Fowl and Jones do not accept the universal, invariant moral principles of Kantian ethics, but they see moral standards as necessary means for tradition-based communities to form character. "Moral rules embody the wisdom of a tradition over time. They are thus contextualized within the friendships and practices of particular communities. The obligations specified by those rules are the obligations required by the exercise of the virtues of character."[20] New situations will call for reinterpretation of moral standards by persons of practical wisdom in the community.

Hauerwas has had a running debate with Roman Catholic moralists on the subject of natural law, which he suspects of ignoring the situated character of every morality. They primarily focus on building bridges to nonbelievers of good will through a language of common human values and rights. Hauerwas contends that, although there is some common ground between different moral traditions, the most effective witness the Church can make is by proclaiming its distinctive story and forming an alternative way of life. He suspects natural law reasoning because it begins from human desires and rationality which cannot indicate what true fulfillment is. Because the true fulfillment of humans is eschatological, creation is the wrong foundation for Christian ethics. "The kingdom does not start with nature, with the notion that the perfection implicit in creation be reformed by divine assistance; rather the kingdom starts as the hope of a people called by God, which for Christians is defined by the life and death of the crucified Christ."[21] He criticizes recent Protestant Christian ethicists for adopting secular moral philosophy's terms and downplaying biblical language in order to make their arguments more intelligible to the larger world. The task of Christian ethics is not "to write as though Christian commitments make no difference in the sense that they only underwrite what everyone already in principle can know, but rather to show the difference these commitments make."[22] This argument raises the larger question of whether the community's story can be shown to be true, and not only helpful for forming a common life.

Testing the Community's Story

Hauerwas usually defends the truth of the Christian narrative in pragmatic terms: the ultimate public test of a true theory is the results which it can produce. The story of a community is adequate if it encourages the members of the community to face the particular challenges and tragedies of life. But this pragmatic test is not the only one. Christians believe the story of Jesus not only because it organizes life in a functional way but because it is true. Because there is no neutral standpoint from which we can objectively assess other traditions, truthfulness for Hauerwas is intimately linked to self-understanding and the conduct that flows from it. He insists that many stories promote self-deception by obscuring the tragedy and compromising nature of our lives. The story of Jesus, which asserts the necessity of the cross, is the one best able to shape a self capable of facing such unpleasant truths.

Recently, serious challenges have been posed to the way narrative theology asserts the truth of the Christian story. What sort of truth should we expect in the assertions of faith communities? Is it sufficient to say that believers find these beliefs *meaningful* in the sense that they impart order and richness to their lives? Must they also be shown to be *true*, in other words, validated in ways which any reasonable person could understand? Some critics insist that unless this standard is met the intellectual honesty of believers is suspect. "Truth" would be no more than whatever a group claims it to be. Hauerwas and many other narrative theologians reply that no one can adequately assess the truth of a world view without participating in a community which embodies that way of life. In the final analysis the truth of a way of life is decided by examples rather than by theoretical arguments. We need to look to specific persons in order to evaluate competing stories, because, as Hauerwas says, "the test of each story is the sort of person it shapes."[23]

Paul Lauritzen charges that the appeal to narratives does not work even within Christian circles. Both Hauerwas and Johannes Metz appeal to narrative to ground the truthfulness of the distinctive Christian vision. They hold that Christian stories and the convictions they engender are justified practically insofar as they produce communities of faith committed to embody their transforming power. Lauritzen, however, points out that the two authors derive opposing strategies of life from the same stories. "For Metz, the result is a life committed to near revolutionary social action; for Hauerwas, a life given to a sort of sectarian pacifistic witness."[24] This sharp divergence signals trouble for a pragmatic justification of the Christian story. "For if the truthfulness of the Christian story is to be judged by its practical consequences, and these consequences are as varied as Hauerwas' and Metz's writings would suggest, how does an appeal to narrative establish the truthfulness of Christian convictions, even on pragmatic grounds?"[25] Lauritzen concludes that the pragmatic demonstration does not work even within the community of belief, let alone before a secular audience. In reply to a similar charge from James Gustafson, Hauerwas wrote that "theological convictions inextricably involve truth-claims that are in principle open to challenge." He insists, however, that a confessional standpoint is necessary to judge these claims: "...the very content of Christian convictions requires that the self be transformed if we are adequately to see the truth of the convictions—e.g., that I am a creature of a good creator yet in rebellion against my status as such."[26]

Paul Nelson's *Narrative and Morality: A Theological Inquiry* gives at least part of the answer to Lauritzen's challenge.[27] Narrative may be indispensable for doing Christian ethics but that does not mean that it is the only resource. Nelson writes that "narrative is necessary but insufficient for Christian ethics. To describe the moral realm as an interweaving of narrative-dependent and narrative-independent features does not nullify the distinctive contribution of narrative to the texture of the Christian moral life."[28] In addition, he points out two obstacles that prevent narrative from solving all theological disagreements. First, Scripture contains an irreducible plurality of narratives that require selection based on non-narrative grounds. Hence, attention to different narratives within scripture may yield discrepant conclusions. Second, the same narrative or biblical narrative as a whole can be interpreted in different ways and used to warrant a variety of substantive theological proposals.[29]

The different interpretations given to the basic Christian story by Metz and Hauerwas can be traced to their ecclesiologies and theories of grace and human nature. Metz's Catholic tradition favors closer ties between Church and culture via natural law ethics and accommodates NT pacifism to contemporary political strife through the just war tradition. These factors lead to a different interpretation of the gospel narrative and its application to questions of violence than the one proposed by Hauerwas. Nevertheless, either theologian ought to provide a rational defense for his ecclesiology and that defense should in principle be open to challenge from other theologians. To favor a confessional perspective does not mean abandoning rationality.

II. Parable: The Gospel in Cameo

The study of parables as a literary and theological genre offers one way through this conflict between universal truths and particular stories. Literature reminds us that not all truths are abstract universals nor are all particulars data which lack sufficient generality to be considered "true." Literary symbols, events, parables and stories are true in a different way than the conclusions of arguments. They are "informative particulars" that embody a moral or religious message. They are not meant to illustrate a point already established in theory or motivational appeals to support general moral principles. The Exodus narrative and the parable of the Good Samaritan, for example, reveal fundamental patterns of religious meaning through their dramatic movement and interaction of characters. Abstracting these religious insights from parable and story deprives them of much of their meaning and capacity to transform the agent. William Wimsatt coined the term "*concrete universal*" to describe a work of literature or art that presents "an object which in a mysterious and special way is both highly general and highly particular."[30] Biblical images and narratives are concrete universals because they are simultaneously general and particular. Their particular narrative form and wealth of detail shape the self-understanding of moral agents, fix distinctive angles of vision on the world, and indicate conduct that is appropriate to their meaning.

John R. Donahue shows how the parables work to shape the morality of the audience. He cites C.H. Dodd's classic definition: "At its simplest the parable is a metaphor or simile drawn from nature or common life, arresting the hearer by its vividness or strangeness, and leaving the mind in sufficient doubt about its precise application to tease it into active thought."[31] The parables of Jesus have four characteristics: they are realistic, metaphorical, paradoxical or surprising, and open-ended. While myths establish a world, parables subvert our ordinary expectations. The reader can become caught by listening attentively to a parable. When this engagement occurs, we do not interpret parables so much as they interpret us. They make us recognize more about ourselves then we care to. Donahue describes how a gospel parable turns the tables on the readers:

> The parable of the Two Debtors which Jesus tells to Simon the Pharisee (Luke 7:41–43) functions in similar fashion as a trap and elicits a grudging acceptance from Simon. So too today, when we read the parable of the Pharisee and the Tax Collector (Luke 18:9–14) and smugly identify with the humble prayer of the tax collector, we are in effect adopting the attitude of the Pharisee, "I am not like others" (Luke 18:11, au. trans.).[32]

Metaphor and story can subvert our settled notions of who we are and how the world always runs. Revelation occurs in the moment when God's action breaks into the realism of the parable. It cracks the shell of "business as usual" and forces us to imagine that we can be different if the Reign of God is drawing near. Because the parables are open-ended, they do not allow the hearer to remain aloof or inactive. They do not tell us what to do because "as religious language they present not simply a series of ethical paradigms or exhortations, though they are often so interpreted, but a *vision of reality which becomes a presupposition to ethics*."[33] Parables indicate that Scripture offers "revealed reality" more than "a revealed morality," as James Gustafson puts it.[34]

The parables have lost much of their revelatory potential because moralizing preachers have tamed these disruptive vignettes into clichés. Too often they have neutralized their impact as metaphors by distilling off a "lesson." We need to recapture the parables' tension and surprise by studying their details and following their dramatic unfolding. As George Stroup describes it, revelation comes not in a "fusion of horizons" between the worlds of parable and hearer but in a "collision of horizons."[35] Donahue traces how the dramatic action of the Good Samaritan parable refuses to permit the audience or the lawyer to set limits on who must be loved; it turns the tables on any attempt to circumscribe the scope of compassion. "Under Luke's tutelage the parable becomes *a paradigm of the compassionate vision* which is the presupposition for ethical action."[36]

The parables function as the gospel in cameo because like Jesus they point beyond their concreteness "to the ultimate mystery of the divine-human encounter."[37] Donahue disagrees with literary critics who locate the transformative power of the parables in the metaphorical process itself. The parables are narratives in metaphoric form which refer to another realm beyond themselves. Those who seem to imagine that "salvation comes from metaphor alone" ignore the one who is speaking these metaphors. "Jesus' language is powerful, not because of its aesthetic brilliance or paradoxical quality, but because of the experience of God it mediates and the kind of life Jesus himself lived. What he spoke of in parable he lived. For example, one can think of his association with tax collectors, sinners, and other marginal groups as an enacted parable of the Lost Sheep (Luke 15:1–7)."[38]

Sallie McFague describes the way metaphors work on the imagination to spark insight. "The response to a metaphor is similar to the response to a riddle: one 'gets' it or not, and what one 'gets' is the new, extended meaning which is a result of the interaction of the subjects."[39] In the metaphorical statement "war is a chess game," for example, both sets of connotations interact to spark an insight. If we take the statement literally, the interaction and the insight both vanish. McFague writes,

As Ricoeur has said perceptively, the interactive partners in permanent tension in a parable are two ways of being in the world, one of which is the conventional way and the other, the way of the kingdom…. The plot of the parable forms one partner of the interactive metaphor while the conventional context against which it is set is the other partner. Reality is redescribed through the tension generated by these two perspectives.[40]

Robert W. Funk describes the revelatory tension between the mundane foreground of the parable and the background of the Reign of God. The parable of the Laborers in the Vineyard (Matt 20:1–16) displays two radically different ways of relating to others and simultaneously discloses the tension between the logic of merit and the logic of grace.[41]

Parables Interpret the Interpreter

Let us see how a parable gets applied to the moral life. It works on the reader to challenge basic moral presuppositions and self-understanding. In Matthew 13, Jesus states: "Again the kingdom of heaven is like a merchant searching for fine pearls. When he finds a pearl of great price, he goes and sells all that he has and buys it" (45–46). If I take this expression literally, I miss the point. I have to enter imaginatively into this brief drama and participate in its movement. I can understand how a shrewd merchant would take a plunge like this, sell everything and borrow whatever he needed to acquire the one pearl that could make his fortune.

This parable turns out to be a dangerous experiment if I get caught up in its logic: it states indirectly that the Reign of God is priceless but can only be attained by spending all that I have upon it. When I reach such a conclusion, I am no longer interpreting the parable; it is interpreting me. It leads me to commitment by exposing my lack of commitment. I have to acknowledge that being a disciple of Jesus is an important value in my life, but not my only allegiance. I have some "side bets" out just in case, a diversified portfolio for my investments. Granted, it makes sense for this merchant who is sure about the pearl to risk everything to acquire it. Does my hedging mean that I don't estimate God's Reign so highly? Or does it expose a fatal cowardice? Without selling everything, that pearl would elude the merchant. Is it the same with me and the Reign of God? These two verses of Scripture which seemed so innocuous at first glance become utterly demanding when I enter into the metaphor and let it shock me into new awareness of my own compromises, which it unmasks as cowardice and stupidity. It is no wonder that Jesus irritated so many of his hearers. On the other hand, the parable is good news as well as demand. Through the logic of the imagination it moves me from what is to what might be. If that merchant could muster the courage to lose all in order to gain all, might I not be able to do the same? Parables are destroyed by moralizing. By reducing the parable to a "moral" I avoid the imaginative involvement which could change my life.

The parables present the presuppositions of New Testament morality rather than constitute that morality itself. They expose our distance from the Reign of God and God's willingness to bridge that distance. As such, they are the flash points of revelation, the literary form through which the Kingdom's logic can burst into our lives. Parables and narratives, however, need to be supplemented by symbol, command, doctrine and the other resources found in Scripture and elsewhere in order to make a full moral argument. When Paul wrestles with the pastoral problems of his congregations, he constantly gravitates toward the central metaphor for the Christian journey, the cross and resurrection of Jesus, but he still employs an entire arsenal of moral equipment, from analogy to moral norms, to specify practical Christian conduct.

Narrative theology operates closer to the fabric of Christian moral experience than most speculative theologies. It broadens the definition of ethics to include the normative guidance that symbolic material brings to disposition and character. Appeals to a common Christian story will not settle every question in moral theology. Nevertheless, narrative theology is a promising development in contemporary theology even though it has not fully explained how it makes its conclusions intelligible to those who have different stories. Perhaps in a pluralistic culture we need to see the resemblances between moral traditions rather than try to rise above them to a neutral common language. The variety of moral perspectives is fed by different imaginative and symbolic traditions that lead to different definitions of the moral issues involved. Those who ignore the aesthetic dimension cut theology off from its deepest religious roots. The next chapter will address the way in which moral dispositions and values are shaped by biblical symbols and stories.

5
Scripture as Basis for Responding Love

This chapter presents a constructive argument for a different approach for using Scripture in ethics which should supplement the previous models. It builds on the work of the narrative theologians but broadens the selection beyond story to include biblical symbols, mandates, and terms of address for God. It answers the moral question, "What ought I to do?" by replying, "Love others as God has loved you in Jesus Christ." Christian moral life has the character of *response* because God's love comes to us first and our actions correspond to the character of that love. Christian love finds the motive and norm for loving others in the story of Jesus which defines the way God continues to love each of us. Christian moral reflection moves from patterns that are central to biblical narrative by analogy to discern appropriate ways of being and acting in the present situation. The love which is the central norm for the Christian life is not an abstract principle but an experience that has a definite shape or *pattern*. That pattern is specified in the story of Jesus and other biblical symbols which enable us to interpret our own experience to recognize the same Lord who is described in the biblical material. Christians experience God's distinctive way of loving as manifested in the history of Jesus Christ and continued through his Spirit in the believing community. Even though God's love is usually mediated through human encounters, faith discerns in those interactions the creative and redemptive presence of God. Scripture is not primarily a record of past experiences of God's love but the means through which we discern how God loves us now in Christ Jesus.

This model of responding love rests on a confessional position: present-day persons can and do experience a love akin to what the original disciples did because Jesus of Nazareth is now the risen Christ. Empowered by this contemporary love of Christ present through the Spirit, they are called to respond by loving others in ways that are analogous to the love they have and continue to receive. As I understand Christian faith, Jesus is believed to be the definitive but not the exclusive revelation of God. As the Epistle to the Hebrew states, "In times past, God spoke in fragmentary and varied ways to [us] through the prophets; in this, the final age, God has spoken to us through his son....This Son is the reflection of the Father's glory, the exact representation of the Father's being" (Heb 1:1-3). Theologically, this confession means that for Christians Jesus Christ is the one to whom the revelations of other traditions point. Morally, it means that Jesus Christ plays a normative role in Christians' moral reflection through the "analogy of experience." There are elements in the contemporary experience of individuals and the Christian community which are sufficiently like the original to enable us to identify with that reality and also elements sufficiently different that we can appropriate it creatively. The biblical story enables us to recognize *which* features of experience are significant, guides *how* we act, and forms *who* we are in the community of faith. We will investigate each of these modes in the discussion that follows.

How can an individual history be normative for a way of life? The major challenge here is to describe conceptually how the person of Jesus Christ can serve as the guiding norm for Christian experience and moral practice. That challenge is set for us by the New Testament, most directly in the new commandment of Jesus in John 13:34 where Jesus tells his disciples in the context of their final meal together, "As I have loved you, so you also should love one another." Although no single verse can capture the rich diversity of the moral teachings of Scripture, this principle is perhaps the most comprehensive statement of NT ethics. Not only the original disciples, but all subsequent Christians are commanded to love one another as Jesus has loved us. Paul makes a similar appeal to the basic pattern of the life, death and resurrection of Jesus when he exhorts the Philippians to mutual respect and service in

Phil 2:1–11: "Have among yourselves the same attitude that is also yours in Christ Jesus" (2:5).

These commandments would make no sense unless there were some basic continuity between the experience of the first disciples and Christians today. Contemporary Christians certainly share the same humanity and thereby stand in continuity with the first generation. They also believe that they stand in the same covenanted community which draws from its memory a sense of identification with the first generation. This sense of historical identification is similar to that of the people of Israel who were exhorted that they too were included in the original covenant event. ("But it is not with you alone that I am making this covenant…it is just as much with those who are not here among us today as it is with those of us who are now here present before the Lord, or God" (Dt 29:13–14). Although the connection based on dynamic community memory is important, however, it is not the central link. More significant is the continuity of experience made possible by the resurrection. Christians believe that Jesus of Nazareth now lives as the Risen Christ and that each generation experiences the same One who continues to reveal God, proclaim the breaking in of God's Reign, heal, forgive and save in the same ways that the gospels relate. NT scholar John P. Meier expresses this central presupposition: "The object of Christian faith is a living person, Jesus Christ, who fully entered into a true human existence on earth in the first century A.D., but now lives risen and glorified, forever in the Father's presence. Primarily, Christian faith affirms and adheres to this person—indeed incarnate, crucified, and risen—and only secondarily to ideas and affirmations about him."[1] The basic pattern of Christian love, therefore, is derived from the person of Jesus Christ who continues to shape the lives of his disciples through their imagination, deepest emotions (affections), and rationality, all of which play a role in discerning ways of acting and living that are analogous to the love of Christ. In briefer form, this model of responding love considers how to obey the command Jesus frequently used to close a parable: "Go and do likewise."

The New Commandment of Jesus

Let us first turn to the specific context of the new commandment of Jesus to examine how Jesus exemplifies it in John's account. The narrative of the foot-washing acts out parabolically the meaning of this distinctive new command. It is the Gospel in cameo since it succinctly expresses the meaning of Jesus' mission in a concrete action set against the backdrop of the Reign of God. The new commandment has a distinctive reference to the person of Jesus that is not found in the two great commandments to love God and neighbor. It reads in the New American Bible translation, "I give you a new commandment: Love one another. Such as my love has been for you, so must your love be for each other. This is how all will know you for my disciples: your love for one another" (13:34–35). The pattern of Jesus' love for them should guide and empower them to love others in analogous ways. Their love continues the mission of Jesus' life because it will extend his love into the world through word and deed so that others will come into the saving relation of faith and friendship with God. The specific history of Jesus is central since the disciples' memory harkens back to it and their mission extends it into the future.

Jesus' statement of the new commandment explains his action of washing the disciples' feet like a slave. This paradoxical action, which confounds the disciples, reveals the significance of the tragic events that were about to unfold. Placed at this pivotal position in the structure of John's gospel, the washing of the feet interprets both the public ministry and the impending passion. Jesus seems to be pulling the reluctant disciples into the drama. They must allow Jesus to perform this service; Peter's protests cannot exempt him from it. Once they have been served in this way by Jesus their own lives are irrevocably implicated. "But if I washed your feet—I who am Teacher and Lord—then you must wash each other's feet. What I just did was to give you an example: as I have done, so you must do. I solemnly assure you, no slave is greater than his master..." (13:14–16). Once the master has become a servant for them, they must be servants to others or else they lose connection with him. That service of Jesus, summed up in the act of footwashing, must become the norm of their lives.

The eucharistic meal and the washing of feet become paradigms for Christian life. They set patterns which will be applied analogously in countless new situations. The pattern is what becomes normative rather than any lesson about humility or equality which might be distilled from the memory of footwashing and the image of Jesus who come not to be served but to serve. Certainly the disciples did not understand the mandate as a demand for external copying. Eucharist, not foot-washing, became the central commemorative ritual of the post-resurrection community.

The new commandment goes *beyond imitation to participation* in two interrelated ways, a union of life and mission. In the first place, Christians' service evolves out of participation in the life of Christ as they enter into the same humiliation and exaltation he underwent. They are called to embody a particular life which now vivifies them through the gift of the Spirit, organically connecting them to Jesus as branches to a vine (Jn 15). They are not called to embody an abstract principle or a set of values, but a distinctive existence. If there is conscious imitation, it will stem from this participation and emerge from within, from the Spirit that conforms the disciples' lives to that of the Master. They are empowered to live a new way of life by the Spirit which dwells within them and their community. Secondly, they take part in the *mission* of Jesus. Their response is not primarily directed back in memory to an historical event. In John's gospel, Jesus does not say, "As I have loved you, so you should love me in return." Gratitude leads the disciples forward into the same mission of Jesus, not backward into nostalgia. They will participate in the life of Jesus if they participate in his mission. The new commandment leads to a mission, as the following verse makes clear: "This is how all will know that you are my disciples, if you have love for one another" (13:35). The words of the risen Jesus to the disciples on Easter eve connects the gift of life with the responsibility for mission because the Spirit which sent Jesus forth now sends them forth: "As the Father has sent me, so I send you. And when he had said this, he breathed on them and said to them, 'Receive the Holy Spirit'" (Jn 20:21–22). The sending of the disciples to bring all into unity with God parallels their mission in the Synoptics to proclaim the Reign of God. The "abundant life" Jesus brings in John's gospel is the eschatological existence heralded by the breaking in of the Reign of God.

Jesus the Concrete Universal for Christian Moral Life

How is Jesus normative for Christian moral living? Whenever Christians seek to understand the fullness of Jesus Christ, they go back to Jesus of Nazareth.[2] They discover in the particular story of this historical figure the one whom the abstractions of Christology often obscure. Contemporary Christologies from below have grounded their investigations in the specific stories of the gospels. Recently, moral theologians are taking a similar turn to answer the question of how Jesus is morally significant for Christians today. I propose that the entire story of Jesus is normative for Christian ethics as its *concrete universal*. William Wimsatt describes the concrete universal as a work of art or literature which presents "an object which in a mysterious and special way is both highly general and highly particular."[3] Jesus is not the only norm of Christian ethics because human nature, practical effectiveness, accurate descriptions of data, and the accumulated wisdom of the tradition are also normative. Nevertheless, whatever actions and dispositions these other sources suggest must be compatible with the basic patterns inherent in the story of Jesus. In addition, Jesus as concrete universal may mandate certain actions and dispositions, like forgiveness of enemies, to which the other sources would not give the same importance. Jesus functions normatively in Christian ethics through the paradigmatic imagination and moral discernment, which are distinctive ways of exercising moral authority.

The greatest challenge to having Jesus function as a moral norm is epistemological: how can a particular life have universal significance? We tend to associate universality with abstract terms and general propositions like the requirement of justice that equals should be treated equally. Because this norm is abstract and general, we expect it to be able to measure any particular situation where fairness is at issue. No abstract formula, however, can comprehend Jesus of Nazareth because his significance inheres in a particular life. The new commandment of John 13 refers back to the full life and ministry of Jesus. The truth which he discloses has universal significance which comes not by way of theory or logical necessity but by plunging into the depths of those particulars. His meaning is inseparable from his story; it resides in the full range of encounters, personalities, and deeds which the gospels relate.[4]

In recent decades theologians have selected literary categories to articulate the concrete meaning of the story of Jesus and Israel: metaphor, symbol, parable, biography, and narrative have all had their turn. Discussion recurs around certain descriptions of Jesus' moral impact: he shapes or informs Christian action which conforms to, corresponds to, or embodies aspects of his life.[5] All these verbs express the activity of *patterning*, of extending to new material the shape which was inherent in an original. The response is guided by the original. The distinctive arrangement of elements in the religious original serves as paradigm, exemplar, prototype, and precedent to guide the actions and dispositions of Christians in new situations. Because biblical patterns combine a stable core with an indeterminate, open-ended dimension, the moral response can be both creative and faithful. We extend a pattern by *analogy* since we move from the recognizable shape in the first instance to novel situations within certain limitations.[6] Mark Twain remarked that history does not repeat itself but it does rhyme. Catching that rhyme is the business of analogical reflection, the process in which experience jells into usable patterns. This exercise of the imagination has two features:

1. A pattern in the original instance that is partly determinate and partly indeterminate.
2. Some process for extending it to novel situations.

Analogical imagination requires a creative transfer because, like the exodus and the exile, the gospel events and teachings are *historical prototypes* rather than *mythical archetypes*, as Elisabeth Schussler Fiorenza has written.[7] The new response harmonizes with the prototype, but in order to be responsive to the actual needs of the day, it cannot copy the original as if it were a completely determined archetype. A paradigm is "a normative exemplar of constitutive structure" but it always has an indeterminate, open-ended dimension.[8] Michael Walzer, for example, argues that the pattern of Exodus has been prototypical for Western political experience. Even groups which did not believe in God found that the liberation from Egypt disclosed the pattern of their own struggles. The meaning and possibility of politics in the West has its proper form:

—first, that wherever you live, it is probably Egypt;
—second, that there is a better place, a world more attractive, a promised land;
—and third, that "the way to the land is through the wilderness." There is no way to get from here to there except by joining together and marching.[9]

The paradigm is an image, a selective but partial aspect; it is not a "mythical archetype" or an exhaustive picture to be replicated in every detail. As Walzer explains, "It isn't only the case that events fall, almost naturally, into an Exodus shape; we work actively to give them that shape. We complain about oppression; we hope (against all the odds of human history) for deliverance; we join in covenants and constitutions; we aim at a new and better social order."[10]

Perhaps this open ended aspect of paradigms explains why the Reign of God and the Spirit remain undefined in the Gospels: they are the dynamic, open dimensions of the action of God which shatter the established order. Nevertheless, they remain connected with the Jesus of the Gospels: his life both announces and exemplifies the Reign of God; the elusive Spirit instills in the disciples "the mind of Christ" (1 Cor 2:16), the dispositions and values of Jesus, as it animates the communal body of Christ. Since Jesus participates in the Reign of God and Spirit, Christians should avoid using him an icon to be reproduced.

If moral knowing is universal and necessary, how can a particular pattern or story be morally normative? Albert R. Jonsen and Stephen Toulmin's study of casuistry argues persuasively that moral knowledge is essentially particular. Particulars are the basis of ethics, not universals. Moral concepts derive from patterns in particular experiences; moral reflection moves analogically from paradigmatic cases to more problematic ones that contain novel elements; and moral wisdom rests more on discerning sensibility than deductive acumen. Practical reasoning actually emulates the practice of good physicians who know the central repository of typical medical conditions and use them as paradigms to diagnose and treat particular patients:

> Medical students and interns in training are shown cases that exemplify the constellations of symptoms, or "syndromes," typical of these varied conditions. In this way they learn what to look for as indicative of any specific condition and so how to recognize it if it turns up again on a later occasion. The key element in diagnosis is thus "syndrome recognition": a capacity to *re*-identify, in fresh cases, a disability, disease, or injury one has encountered (or read about) in earlier instances.[11]

Medicine and ethics move from paradigmatic cases to problematic ones by *analogical reflection* which detects familiar patterns in novel circumstances. Those who expect highly exact, universal and invariant judgments from either discipline forget that medical students learn to become physicians by making hospital rounds, not by performing laboratory analyses of chemical compounds.

I propose that Jesus of Nazareth functions normatively as a **concrete universal**, because his particular story embodies a paradigmatic pattern which has universal moral applicability. (Similarly, the exodus event is the concrete universal which is normative for ethics in the Jewish tradition.) Christians move imaginatively from his story to their new situation by analogical reasoning. The concrete universal guides three phases of moral experience: perception, motivation, and identity since it indicates

1. *which* particular features of our situation are religiously and morally significant;
2. *how* we are to act even when *what* we should do is unclear;
3. *who* we are to become as a people and as individuals.

I. Discerning the Patterns in Experience

First, let us consider how concrete universals guide us to perceive *which* features of experience are significant. Consider the role of vision and attention in morality: Why did Plato and Aristotle fail to notice the plight of the poor of Athens when Isaiah and Jeremiah focused so intensely on the poor of Israel? The prophets made treatment of the poor the measure of Israel's moral performance. The difference between the Athenian philosophers and the prophets of Israel does not stem from intelligence but from their imaginations and vision. The paradigms of an insistent tradition sharpened the vision of the prophets. They paid attention to the widow, the orphan, and the immigrant workers out of Israel's central exemplary memory. They caught the rhyme between their liberation from Egypt and the need of the marginated in subsequent eras. Through the lens of the Exodus paradigm, its beneficiaries could recognize their obligation to "Go and do likewise" in turn. Note the illuminating power of the paradigmatic imagination: they *saw* the poor because they *saw* them *as* fellow sufferers who were likewise dear to the God of Israel. By contrast, because Plato and Aristotle did not *see* the poor *as* morally significant, they did not *see* them at all. The Homeric and tragic traditions of Greece contained no exemplary memories which would enable the philosophers to recognize barbarians, slaves, women or the poor as worthy of moral consideration, let alone as moral agents.

Moral recognition is a special case of perception in general. We only *perceive* what we *perceive as* something. Garret Green calls the little word "as" "the copula of the imagination" because it defines the selective and interpretive role of imagination. "We always see something by recognizing that it is *like* something else; that is, we always see according to some paradigm."[12] The paradigmatic imagination is precisely the ability to see one thing *as another*. Gestalt psychologists hold that all perception is patterned because we grasp sense data as arranged, as wholes before we distinguish the individual parts. Just as we read units of print as words and phrases, not as individual letters that then get composed into words, so we do not first apprehend sense data and then compose it interpretively into perceptual patterns. Perceptual wholes are not merely the sum of their parts but patterns set by language, memory, and custom which are the arrangements in which data is initially apprehended. If our initial take on perception proves inadequate, we have to modify these presumptive categories.

Religious experience is selective insofar as it relies on communal paradigms to notice which features are significant. As Green describes it, "The Scriptures are not something we look *at* but rather look *through*, lenses that focus what we see into an intelligible pattern."[13] Biblical patterns, however, are paradigms, not icons. Analogical reflection helps Christians spot the rhyme between Jesus' story and their own. To put it starkly, we are called to follow Jesus, not to imitate him. The danger of some "imitation of Christ" spiritualities is that they terminate in the person of Jesus, like worshipping an icon, whereas the Jesus of the gospels was radically concerned about God and about the poor, the outcast, the sinner. To be a disciple of Jesus is to take seriously what he took seriously. What Jesus took seriously was not himself but the breaking in of the Reign of God and the people most in need of justice and reconciliation. Jesus in the Gospels does not draw attention to himself but to the action of God in their midst. So to take Jesus seriously is not to imitate his actions and attitudes because he acted that way, but because these are the ways to heal the world, reconcile enemies, and transform oppression into justice.

Protestants tend to prefer the language of "following Christ" to "imitating Christ" in order to make the distance between master and disciple clear. James Gustafson writes that when the proper qualifications are observed, biblical ethics can be described formally as "the imitation of God." In Old Testament language this is expressed "Be holy as I am, says the Lord"; "Your attitude must be that of Christ" captures it in the New (Phil 2:5). Love responds to an a free initiative of God that instructs and empowers a response that is "in the shape of the engendering deed." As Gustafson explains, "The form is more like: 'God has done *a*, **b**, and **c** for the well-being of the human community and the whole of creation; those who have experienced the reality of God's *a*, *b*, and **c** are moved and required to do similar things for others."[14] This formulation points the individual back to the tradition that has revealed the distinctive ways of God. These become both motive and norm for a distinctive moral response from those who have been so loved and forgiven. "Go and do likewise" is therefore the most succinct summary of biblical morality.

Test Case: H. Richard Niebuhr's Discernment of God's Action

H. Richard Niebuhr described how biblical symbols can be used to discern which features of experience point to God's present action and our appropriate response. He pointed out the dangers of a Christ-centered piety which made him an exclusive, completely determinate icon.[15] Instead he proposed a form of theological discernment which applies the interpretive powers of the imagination. In objective reasoning our ideas help order the confusing swarm of sense data into intelligible patterns. "By means of ideas we interpret as we sense, and sense as we interpret."[16] Through the imagination we use pertinent symbols and images to decipher the conflicting possibilities presented by our senses. These images are usually mechanical or mathematical when we are thinking about objects. In the personal realm, however, we use images of persons to order the raw data of our affections. "We meet each one," wrote Niebuhr, "with an imagination whereby we supply what is lacking in the immediate datum and are enabled to respond, rightly or wrongly, to a whole of reality of which this affection is for us a symbol and a part."[17] Christians use the life of Jesus Christ as a key image or symbolic form to interpret their experience in light of the framework of God's action and character.

Niebuhr begins from the presupposition that God acts in and through the intentions of finite agents. The believer is called to discern and respond to the creating, judging and redeeming of God. Therefore, before asking, "What ought I to do?" believers should ask, "What is God doing in this situation?" The answer will not come from any direct command of God or from a reasonable assessment of what is normatively human, but from a process of discernment guided by key biblical symbols and perspectives. *Discernment* is an exploratory way of knowing in the concrete which employs imaginative and affective criteria to discover what the appropriate response should be to God's action.

The best known example of Niebuhr's discernment is his series of articles in *The Christian Century* in 1942 and 1943. He asked a question that upset many of the journal's readers: "What is God doing in the war?" The two biblical themes that guided his discernment are indicated in the titles "War as the Judgment of God" and "War as Crucifixion."[18] The biblical symbols of judgment and the cross help to set the point of view for discerning how to respond to God's action, even in such a confusing time as the middle of World War II. Niebuhr turned to the precedent of the prophet Isaiah who tried to make religious sense out of Assyria's invasion of Israel in 701 B.C.E. Even with the army of Sennacherib besieging Jerusalem, the prophet detected a different meaning in the invasion than did the boasting tyrant. The prophet saw that the Lord had a different design. He discounted Sennacherib's arrogance which takes credit for all his success; in truth, the conqueror is merely a tool in the Lord's hands: "Will the axe boast against him who hews with it?...As if a rod could sway him who lifts it, or a staff him who is not wood!" (Is 10:15).

Every event has multiple meanings because it is interpreted from different angles of vision. From the conqueror's standpoint, he is the cause of his own victories; from the cowering Israelites' point of view, he is a threat to national survival; to the prophet, he is the instrument of God's saving judgment on faithless Israel. The prophet has a privileged standpoint because he is committed to pay attention to the action of the one universal Lord in every event of life. Isaiah called for a constructive response to this national emergency because he interpreted the events in a context of faith and saw them as Yahweh's call to Israel to repent and return to the covenant. Niebuhr then moves by analogy to the present crisis of World War II to discover God's healing judgment at work which calls all to repentance rather than self-righteousness. Many Americans and the Allies took the standpoint of retributive justice and saw themselves as punishing unjust and brutal aggressors. Niebuhr pointed out that this crusading mentality rested in part on the illusion that the Allies were doing God's work to punish the guilty. Divine justice, however, "is never merely punishment for sins," he wrote, "as though God were concerned simply to restore the balance between men by making those suffer who have inflicted suffering, but…it is primarily punishment of sinners who are to be chastised and changed in the character which produced the sinful acts."[19]

Viewing the conflict through the symbol of biblical judgment rather than retributive justice, Niebuhr concluded that God was on neither side because the relative culpability of various nations ought not to be judged by humans. If the war were fought under the assumption that the Allies were God's agents of retribution, it would lead to vindictive actions. No wonder his readers objected so strenuously! Instead of citing specific rules to dictate behavior, Niebuhr probed the attitudes of both pacifists and "coercionists" and found them both inadequate. He limited himself to suggesting a theological context for interpreting the war which would lead to a new spirit of prosecuting it. From the perspective of the cross, the fitting response to the suffering of the innocent may well be continuing struggle to defeat the enemy, but tempered by repentance that acknowledged the Allies' complicity in permitting injustice and hope in the renewing action of God who brings possibilities where humans would despair.

II. Scripture Guides How Christians Ought To Act

Next, we move to the question of motivation. As the concrete universal, Jesus indicates *how* to act even when his story does not directly indicate *what* to do. The biblical paradigms become scenarios by motivating believers to act in certain ways that correspond to the paradigms. The paradigms provide motivation in definite directions: they generate *dispositions*, that is, dynamic attitudes that are "disposed" or lean toward acting in certain ways. The affective salience, the emotional energy, engendered through the paradigm translate it into a scenario for corresponding action. Although egotism and sin may cloud or distort the response, the story of the Good Samaritan, for example, disposes those who hear it to notice and act compassionately to those in dire need.

It is obvious that many of the problems we face today have no precedent in biblical literature: global inequity, racism, complex structures of economic exploitation, AIDS, etc. People often question the ethical relevance of Scripture because it does not tell us what to do in these modern dilemmas (even though they are not always willing to accept the explicit mandates of Scripture which do apply today). This is a classic example of "begging the question," that is, it assumes what it intends to demonstrate. The questionable assumption is that the moral life consists in finding and applying specific rules. We must acknowledge that Jesus commands or forbids certain types of actions; he does more than recommend certain attitudes and dispositions. Moral principles, however, do only part of the work of ethics. We rely more on mature character and virtuous habits to recognize what is going on, to appreciate the values involved, the interactions with others, and discern an appropriate response. Accordingly, the formation of character is the most important issue in moral maturation. If we adopt the perspective of virtue and character ethics, Scripture has extensive moral authority but on a different level of experience than the rational application of principles.

Virtue ethics focuses on a pattern of dispositions anchored in the Gospel that guide the moral agent to recognize action which is consonant with the biblical exemplar. Those same dispositions provide the motivation to carry the discernment into action. Biblical paradigms become scenarios for action by evoking affective energies in distinctive ways. Affectivity deteriorates into sentiment when it shuns action. As Oscar Wilde noted, "A sentimentalist is one who desires to have the luxury of an emotion without paying for it."[20] As mentioned above, paradigms become practical in two stages: they contain a discernible pattern which can be noticed elsewhere; second, there are procedures for extending the analogy to new situations. Analogical reflection extends biblical paradigms primarily through dispositions which are configured into a pattern by those original events. Other controls also come into play: ordinary standards of morality, consequences, and community practice among them.[21]

The largely Roman Catholic debate on the distinctiveness of Christian ethics reached a dead end because it concentrated on the *what* of morality to the exclusion of the *how*. The debate got muddled by asking what principles or values obligated Christians that obligated no one else. Since the autonomy school sharply distinguished motive from moral content, it relegated Scripture to providing affective backing to common human values and obligations. Although I would argue that Scripture does mandate certain practices for members of the community of faith which are not necessarily mandatory for all persons, Scripture primarily exerts its normative function by setting a pattern of dispositions rather than dictating directly the content of action.[22] These dispositions (the *how* of morality) then guide the agent to discern *what* to do or forego.

Terry Anderson, the American journalist, illustrates how dispositions engage the Christian imagination. When he was released from seven years of captivity in Lebanon, reporters asked him whether he felt hatred for his captors. He replied, "As a Christian, I am required to forgive my enemies. No, I don't hate them. I am trying to love them." The Hezbollah guerrillas had given him a single book, the Bible, in the first year and he read it cover to cover fifty times. His dormant Christian faith gradually revived and he began to consider his kidnappers as objects of forgiveness rather than resentment. Surely, he read the commandment "love your enemies," but the commandment alone did not shape his response. Multiple metaphors and stories combined to interpret his captors as a special kind of enemy: the image of turning the other cheek, the reaction of Jesus to his enemies, the rebuke of Peter's violent defense, the story of the crucifixion against the background of Isaiah's Servant Songs, Paul's description of the ministry of reconciliation, among others. Taken as a framework, these multiple scenarios converged on a strategy: the appropriately Christian response was forgiveness rather than vindictive retaliation.

The *appropriate response* is the goal of moral reflection. While a virtuous response must be good and right, it should also be appropriate because it is done in the right way to the right person in the right manner and at the right time. Appropriateness indicates that the action is affectively correct, considerate, sensitive, and fitting. A response is appropriate when it fits both underlying scenarios and the situation of action. The relation is triangular: the agent, the actual situation, and culturally learned scenarios of emotion. Ronald de Souza writes, "Paradigm scenarios are the original rituals that give meaning to our present responses, however private. And where there is no adequate original scenario to fall back on, the adult ritual plays much the same function of defining and framing."[23] As noted in our discussion of Hauerwas in the previous chapter, the ritual of the Eucharist has moral implications for the congregation: hospitality, fundamental equality, and peace-making—points made graphically by Paul in chapters eight to eleven of First Corinthians. A single paradigm scenario cannot usually indicate the appropriate response.

We need a variety of perspectives, images, and metaphors to bring out the potential relevance of the objective conditions because they have diverse potentials for interest and value. They call for multiple metaphorical mappings to disclose their affective richness and help imagine a response that will harmonize with our basic convictions. On the other hand, this metaphorical inspection may disclose contradictions between our actions and basic convictions. When Anderson pointed out that the Koran does not allow people to be kidnapped or imprisoned without trial, he confounded and infuriated his Muslim fundamentalist captors. They shouted religious slogans at him since they could not deny the obvious inconsistency between their actions and the paradigms of a just Allah who shows compassion to the defenseless. Similarly, Christian theologies which advocate justice without regard for compassion would be inconsistent with the normative paradigms of the gospel. The early twentieth century labor organizer, Mother Jones, supposedly said, "Until justice is established, there is no time for mercy!" Pitting justice against mercy violates the paradigm scenarios of Jesus's parables and his treatment of persons.

Biblical paradigms provide Christians with scenarios for their emotions and actions. They should meet their adversaries with distinctive perspectives and dispositions that make forgiveness appropriate. As gospel perspectives and ideals become internalized as habits of the heart, this discernment may occur almost unconsciously. According to many spiritualities, the more mature Christian will often realize what to do spontaneously, or at least he or she will screen out intentions that clash with her fundamental convictions. Certain virtues become "connatural" to the person growing in Christian holiness; they are internalized scenarios which convey a readiness to act in certain ways. They can tutor the imagination, making it possible to discern an appropriate response with ease and joy. When we know *how* to act, *what* to do should become clearer.

Scripture, through a gradual process of reflection and assimilation in faith, can engender a distinctive set of affections correlative to its story, which disposes the agent to act in distinctive ways. In *Can Ethics Be Christian?* James M. Gustafson describes how the affections link religious convictions and appropriate moral actions: "Basic is the affirmation that the experience of the reality of God evokes, sustains, and renews certain 'sensibilities' or 'senses,' certain sorts of awareness, certain qualities of the human spirit. These in turn evoke, sustain, and renew moral seriousness and thus provide reasons of the mind and heart for moral life, indeed for a moral life of a qualitatively distinctive sort."[24] Certain moral dispositions correlate with the experiences of God which are named by the images of Scripture; this specific set of affections bridges religious experiences and moral action. Gustafson cites some of the principal affections that Scripture as a whole should engender: a sense of radical dependence, of gratitude, repentance, obligation, possibility and direction. Like a mobile, they are interdependent and reciprocally defining. For example, repentance without a sense of hope and possibility would not be a fitting response to the reality of God as witnessed in the biblical tradition.

Virtuous dispositions must also be appropriate to the particular situation of action as well as to the paradigm scenarios. They enable us to navigate in a particular complex of conditions, intentions, persons, etc. If emotions are at variance with these actualities, we judge them to be inappropriate. How truthful are these dispositions? Are they projections onto experience or do they disclose its hidden depths? Do the symbols of the cross and resurrection of Jesus, for example, reveal in some way the significance of human suffering? This significance will not be grasped theoretically but in recognizing the obscure presence of God who suffers with us. The cross and resurrection will help disclose what is going on at the most ultimate level. When Jeremiah and Isaiah saw the poor *as* the special people of God, they were not seeing them *as if* they were. The memories and images imparted by their tradition enabled them to grasp the true value of the poor. Biblical images can disclose obscure qualities of experience so that we have a more adequate evaluation of what is happening.

Gratitude and Hope: The Path from Memory to Action

Gratitude and hope are the central affections that move us from faith memory to corresponding action. They make the memory of God's gift an empowering source of moral generosity by recognizing that the gift of God requires us to act generously toward others. The new commandment does not turn gratitude back to God or to Jesus, but points to others who should be the beneficiaries of that gratitude. Gratitude stretches forward to advance the Reign of God, motivated by the hope that all will be reconciled in God. The Reformers inveighed against a morality based on expectation of reward, and rightly so: self-interested calculation destroys gratitude and undermines the basis of Christian morality. Just as earning your own keep is the exact opposite of responding to a freely given gift, so too the moral lives based on these two approaches are simply incompatible. We do not move from the indicative of God's gift to the imperative by a logical consistency that follows the Golden Rule. Rather, the link comes by gratitude that turns into active hope and compassion. The love God has shown us in Christ was a merciful attitude directed toward those who were alienated. Gratitude for unexpected gifts evokes a corresponding merciful love toward others and hope of reconciliation with those most distant from us through the work of justice. We come to appreciate "the stranger" in a new way, as the liberation theologians predict will happen when we make an option for the poor based on God's concern for them.

The parable of the unjust steward in Matthew 18:21–35 illustrates how gratitude is the link between grace received and service extended to others. The parable empowers forgiveness of our neighbors by appealing to memory and imagination and not merely to moral logic. The steward does not make the transition from receiving mercy to showing it in the treatment of his fellow servant. Even though he has been forgiven a staggering amount he embezzled, which would have been impossible to repay, he turns around and abuses another servant who owes him a minor sum. The king is outraged not at the steward's inconsistency but at his monstrous ingratitude. There is no comparison between the two debts, and such a great gift of forgiveness should have inspired life-altering gratitude. Love should have engendered love and forgiveness should have led to more forgiveness out of gratitude. If I enter the world of the parable imaginatively and honestly, it discloses much more than the general truth that Christians are called to endless forgiveness because they have been forgiven so much by God. It should also reveal where the logic of vengeance operates in my own relationships and how my resentment is completely out of place with the experience of God's unlimited mercy.

All of the moral imperatives of the Bible are authorized and energized by gratitude for undeserved mercy and love. Gratitude and hope are the obvious expressions of grace received. James Gustafson comments on the biblical maxim, "Freely you have received, freely give." He writes, "The comma, in a sense, covers the fulcrum of a way of life. In its affective dimensions, the sense of gratitude moves the will to act....It is out of a sense of gratitude that both moral volition and an imperative arise. God has freely given life to us; we, in thankfulness to him, are to be concerned for others' well-being as he has been concerned for ours."[25] The memory of grace does not leave one self-satisfied or complacent. It becomes a source of hope through the empowerment which it gives us. Hope is likewise born of compassion for the poor and oppressed when our imagination is guided by the promise of the Reign of God. It is coming, but it requires our wholehearted efforts to alleviate the effects of sin and oppression. Like the promised Kingdom, hope does not amount to a blueprint. Nevertheless, Christian hope is guided by the source of Christian gratitude in remembering the one who announced it. The life and death of Jesus of Nazareth give a historical shape to the breaking Reign of God.

Test Case: Salvadoran Identification with the Cross and Resurrection

Biblical paradigms derive their disclosive power from the belief that God continues to act in the present in the characteristic ways narrated in Scripture. "Paradigms" and "scenario" are terms that may imply that believers resort to the stories and symbols of Scripture as repositories of folk wisdom. In Latin America and other situations of struggle the symbols of faith show a much more profound significance: they enable people to find God and Jesus Christ in the present. The chapel of the Universidad Centro Americana in San Salvador is named for Archbishop Romero. On the outside of the chapel are inscribed his words which were broadcast days before his assassination. "If they kill me, I will rise again in the Salvadoran people." The verb used is *resucitar*, which explicitly means "to resurrect." On the inside of the same wall are the traditional series of fourteen "stations of the cross." However, instead of the customary pictures of the passion of Jesus there are fourteen ink drawings of Salvadoran victims of torture: men, women and children who have been stripped, beaten, mangled and executed. The message of identification is direct: the cross and resurrection of Jesus continue today in the passion and victory of the people of El Salvador. They identify their sufferings with the ongoing Cross and Resurrection, the present action of God in the world as God defeats sin and injustice through the travail of the Body of Christ. They see themselves as making up for what is lacking in the sufferings of Christ by extending his trials and triumph into new times and places.

Jon Sobrino, who teaches at that university, describes the dynamics of Christian solidarity: "It is in virtue of this proximity of Jesus to his own world that he is felt by the poor of Latin America today to be someone who is close to themselves."[26] Notice how the logic of identification operates: as they become aware that Jesus drew close to the poor of his day, the poor of today recognize that he is present to them. They do not merely adopt his story as their own in order to bring meaning to their experience. When they discover that they are part of the continuing story of Jesus the Liberator, that he suffers and dies with them so that they share his new life, that story becomes normative Good News for them. When others join this struggle in an act of solidarity, that also brings them into solidarity with God who continues to act in history through the liberating event of the Cross and Resurrection of Jesus. Sobrino writes:

> God incarnate, incredibly close to the poor, and oppressed in the scandal of the cross, is approached through kinship with God in incarnation among the oppressed of history—in persecution, in the surrender of our very lives with them. The God of hope...of resurrection...is approached by a kinship with God in the stubbornness of hope in, through and against history.[27]

Liberation theologians and the artists who constructed the chapel at the UCA are using the "paradigm scenario" of the crucifixion to urge Christians to identify with Jesus as the religious link between the biblical text and today's crises. The power of the scenario comes from their belief that Jesus continues to work in the world in ways similar to the gospel story.

This line of argument echoes the theological discernment of H. Richard Niebuhr. Although his ethics was radically theocentric and he condemned the use of Jesus as an icon, he recognized the indispensable role that Jesus plays for Christians in construing what was going on. He appealed to the dispositions of Jesus (*how* he acted and related) as a norm for discerning the moral qualities which are operative in a contemporary situation. Jesus is "the symbolic figure" which the Christian uses to test "the spirits to see if among all the forces that move within him, his societies, the human mind itself, there be a uniting, healing, a knowing, a whole-making spirit, a Holy Spirit. And he can do so only with the aid of the image, the symbol of Christ. Is there a Christ-like spirit there?"[28] I interpret Niebuhr to mean that the values of Jesus Christ are linked together by the gospel narratives into a set or constellation which can function as a complex affective norm. The maturing Christian gradually incorporates this set of values into his or her affectivity in such a way that it can function as a "sounding board" for discerning the values in a particular course of action. Does it resonate with those qualities which together constitute what we call the "spirit" of Jesus? Or does the basic affective tone of a situation or action clash with those values so that one concludes, "No, a Christ-like spirit is not present here."

Worship, Contemplation, and Moral Dispositions

How do these virtuous dispositions get incorporated into the character of believers? One of the main ways is through the language of prayer and praise. Doxology, the language of praise, locates the believer in the rhythm of the history of salvation and evokes the affective dispositions to support a life that will witness to the Lord of that history. Scripture "schools" the affections by presenting the various names which the believer uses to address God and the narrative that orders those images into a remembered whole. In our developing life of faith we address God long before we speculate about God. By revealing the appropriate names of God, Scripture instructs our hearts in new ways of relating to God. When we address God using a specific image we are led to assume the affective stance connoted in that image. Whether we address God in direct, second person speech or speak about God in third person predication, a specific affection is usually invoked which invites the speaker to take a definite stance before the Lord.

Psalm 23 shows how the affections are schooled. The invocation "The Lord is my shepherd" should *evoke* the very trust expressed in the rest of the doublet: "there is nothing I shall want" (23:1). This image for God can be authentically spoken only by someone who is willing to stand before God in confident surrender, which may at times be either a rich experience or only a dry, deliberate turning to God. "The Lord is my shepherd" may not stir up particular feelings of trust, but it should always evoke a particular way of standing before the Lord, a disposition and attitude of the heart and will. Scripture, therefore, is normative for the affections of Christian life as they are formed through liturgical prayer and doxology. The names of God and the narrative that holds them together present a distinctive picture of God, the world, and our fellow creatures which enables us to see them in a new light and respond appropriately. Praying "The Lord is my shepherd" will not tell us what to do when we "walk through the valley of darkness," but it can orient us to the One who has promised to accompany us and away from actions that would alienate us from that companionship.

The affections are schooled not only by a biblical vocabulary that liturgical prayer uses to address God, but also by biblical scenes that contemplative prayer savors and relishes. *Contemplation* is the imaginative entry into a particular scene. Every story can become my story through the musing of faith and identification with the characters of the narrative. I identify in mind and heart with the adulterous and repentant David, the irrepressible Bartimaeus who insists on being cured, the swagger and fear of Peter hearing of the impending passion of Jesus. By identifying with their experience based on similar ones of my own, I am also able to identify with their reactions to the words of the Lord—they are spoken to me, too. This is the opposite of play-acting; their cries, prayers and laments turn out to be the most authentic words to voice my own experience. Without this imaginative identification we are but distant spectators on the events of Scripture, and no revelation occurs in our own lives. Being an affectively detached observer promises a false objectivity in studying Scripture. By not acknowledging the gift of grace, it is unlikely that I can appreciate the call which that grace entails. The most thorough study of biblical hermeneutics will come to very little without this imaginative re-entry into the world of the text and engagement with the One it discloses. The critical distance of exegesis can become an unbridgeable gulf between the scholar and the Word of

God. Contemplation encourages the "second naiveté" described by Paul Ricouer; it enables us to return to the text to participate in it, enhanced but not crippled by critical thought.[29]

Liturgical rituals, as well as sound preaching and prayerful contemplation on the incidents of the life of Jesus and the story of Israel, will help evoke characteristically Christian dispositions. Fidelity to acting on them habitually will sharpen an intuitive discernment of actions that correspond to the mind of Christ. Obviously, this growth requires repentance and continuous conversion since bias and sin are never eradicated. Although praxis is the condition for moral insight into the paradigm scenarios, contemplative reflection imprints the scenarios in imagination and affect. The community of faith is the ordinary place where this schooling of the affections takes place.

III. Scripture Shapes Christian Identity

Finally, the story of Jesus is normative for *who* we are to become as Christians, individually and communally. Here too we employ a pattern by analogous reflection. Just as paradigms highlight certain features for moral recognition and scenarios establish a distinctive set of dispositions, narrative forms the normative basis of personal identity. In the latter part of the twentieth century, the question of identity seems to have displaced the issue of purpose as the fundamental moral issue: *why* we do anything gains its meaning from *who* we are, have been, and are becoming.

A mature person is not a bundle of dispositions but possesses a degree of integration which we usually call character. An integrated character is the result of an integrated narrative insofar as the person's identity correlates with a way of life appropriated in his or her own unique way. Biblically informed affections are like elements on a delicately balanced mobile; the framework that keeps them in balanced tension is the overall structure of the story of Israel and Jesus. As Hauerwas and MacIntyre put it, virtues are "narrative-dependent." Specific narrative units help define a given affection or hold together two or more affections in a distinctive configuration. For example, the story of the woman caught in adultery in John 8 shows how Jesus upholds justice and mercy without compromising either; it is doubtful whether any theoretical discussion of the relation of justice and mercy could relate them so well. Anyone who enters into that story imaginatively will discover that in Christ there is no mercy without repentance and no justice without compassion and hope. The specific history of Israel and Jesus taken as a whole provides the dramatic unity for the various qualities of Christian affectivity. Don Saliers, a contemporary American Methodist theologian, writes, "The essential feature of the order among Christian emotions is that they take God and God's acts as their object and their ground."[30] Remembering and confessing these saving acts "schools" the affections by training them to be the qualities which are displayed in the overall biblical narrative.

Contemporary cognitive psychology agrees with narrative theology that humans need a moving dramatic unity, a story with a beginning, middle and end, to bring integrity into their personal histories. No other imaginative device can synthesize our diverse moments of experience into a coherent whole.[31] Truthful narratives indicate that the self is at stake in moral choices. False narratives obscure vital areas of experience and lead to self-defensive scripts in which the self holds center stage. Although culture and traditions supply us with a considerable range of models, metaphors, scenarios and roles, these resources do not hang together without narrative structures, which supply "the most comprehensive synthetic unity that we can achieve."[32] The self emerges through commitment and interpretation made possible by socially derived narratives, and in turn lives out a unique version of them. There are other factors in personal identity as well: principles which can structure a life, commitment to a cause which involves one in a community formed around the same cause, friendship over time, and rituals are just a few of these factors. Nevertheless, narrative seems to be indispensable for a time-filled, coherent self.

Narrative theologians have made the case that the story form of revelation is no accident. The self-disclosure of a personal God in history comes through a story conveyed within communities of memory and hope. One cannot fashion a personal identity around a creed or a set of doctrines. Christian salvation comes through a particular human story which offers a framework extending from birth to death that enables individuals to accept the healing of their fragmentation and betrayals. New Testament moral instruction revolves around this central event where the disciples are to identify with Christ. For example, "Rejoice insofar as you are sharing Christ's sufferings, so that you may also be glad and shout for joy when his glory is revealed" (1 Pet 4:13; see also Phil 2:1–11; Heb 12:1–4). Unfortunately, Christian theology too often has concentrated on the birth and death of Jesus for moral significance, as though what occurred between the Incarnation and the Paschal Mystery served only to fill up the interval.

Although the end of the story provides the definitive vantage point on the life of Jesus, his entire life has normative significance. The new commandment's norm, "as I have loved you," covers the full story. It can guide our response if we can enter imaginatively and faithfully into the scenes and encounters of that history. Recent Christology has unearthed the full humanity of Jesus who struggled with purpose, betrayal, opposition, doubt and failure all in relation to God and the arrival of God's reign. At the same time, the story of Jesus is not so overdetermined that we cannot make it our own. We identify with Jesus not only by taking seriously what he took seriously and acting in ways faithful to his story, but also by identifying with his social reality extended through time and space, the Body of Christ. Because Scripture addresses communities rather than individuals, the appropriate moral response is discerned within the community of faith.[33] The four elements of the hermeneutical process we identified in the introduction are 1) the communities that authored Scripture in relation to 2) the challenges they faced which sets the pattern for the discernment of 3) contemporary communities of faith reflecting on 4) the issues that challenge them today. The central question, therefore, is: How are we to respond to our challenges in ways analogous to the responses which the early Christian communities made to their own challenges as we strive to serve the same Lord?

Jerome Murphy-O'Connor, O.P. reinforces this communal hermeneutic by locating in it the internal religious principle of faithful interpretation, namely, the Spirit of Jesus. The transformation and sanctification of individuals occurs through their incorporation into the local instance of the Body of Christ. Ephesians 4 stresses that the "new humanity" being formed in the world is identical with the communal Christ. While individuals are given different gifts of the Spirit to serve, it is the community as a whole that is called to image forth the contemporary reality of Christ. Murphy-O'Connor writes, "As the community deepens its commitment to the ideal, the existential attitude of Christ (cf. Phil 2:5) becomes progressively more manifest, primarily in the community and derivatively in the individuals who constitute it. To the extent that the community exemplifies the authentic humanity manifested by Christ, it judges from the standpoint of Christ. It is in this sense that it can be said to possess 'the mind of Christ.'"[34] The community internalizes the values of Christ through the Spirit of Jesus so that, as it matures, it comes closer to following the fundamental norm of Christian morality, the person of Jesus Christ. To the extent that the community is faithful to the Spirit, it mediates to its members this "mind of Christ" as normative for their own formation of character and moral decisions. Conversely, to the extent that the community is unfaithful, it mediates to its members the false stories it has uncritically absorbed from the culture at large or perpetuated through its self-absorbed "traditions."

The biblical narrative prototype itself is open to revision, as Paul's ministry to the Gentiles proves. Those revisions are often interpreted as unwelcome innovations, a reaction reminiscent of the first great Christian innovation when the apostle James and the Jerusalem community resisted Paul's baptism of gentiles (see Galatians 2; Acts 15). Prototypes undergo development when they are applied to new situations, and these new applications bring out aspects that were latent in the original or even at variance with its presuppositions. This holds for both moral and religious prototypes.[35] Radically new situations can lead to significant revision of biblical exemplars. For example, Phyllis Trible and other feminist theologians have reinterpreted the Genesis accounts in light of the contemporary experience of women to bring out its message of equality to which patriarchal interpretations had been blind.[36] Reading the biblical stories through distorted lenses highlights the wrong aspects of the pattern and invites deceptive construals of what is going on in the present. Feminist and womanist theologians have eloquently shown how sexism, racism and classism have used the story of Jesus in oppressive ways. Some correct the prototype by retrieving other biblical patterns which counteract these distortions.[37] If Jesus acted against the unjust structures and exclusive practices of his day, then Christians must do so today.

Controls on Using the Images, Affections and Stories of Scripture

How do we select the right biblical images, affections and stories for moral guidance? Any appeal to analogy has to observe certain standards so that the original or "prime analogate" controls the application in contemporary practice. Otherwise, the biblical material will not be a prototype but only a decoration to the author's presentations. Scripture then would have no genuine authority but be used dishonestly to give the impression that it endorses whatever the author is advocating. Some current writers seem to have abandoned proof-texting for "proof-theming," that is, selecting biblical images that support moral conclusions which they have reached on other grounds. History has shown that fanatics often cloak their delusions in the mantle of inspiration by appealing to convenient biblical precedents. Michael Walzer relates how the Exodus account has inspired "messianic politics" which tries to bring history to a climax by "forcing the End." People are tempted to create their own deliverance from evil. "They claim divine authority for their politics and effectively rule out the requirements of both morality and prudence."[38] Why not imitate Samson's destruction of the Philistines by terrorist tactics rather than Moses' deliverance of the people from slavery, since both are found in the canonical Scripture? What criteria can prevent the all too familiar corruptions of biblical discernment?

There are several criteria, though none are foolproof:

1. *Centrality of the Image or Story.* The appropriate biblical images should be central to the canon of Scripture. Did they function as continuing sources of revelation for the tradition or are they at least consistent with its central images? The exodus, for example, continued to shape Israel's consciousness, while on the other hand the holy war of total annihilation related in Judges did not play this role.

2. *Theological Soundness.* The guiding images should convey or be coordinate with a theologically sound image of God. The exodus implies the character of God as Redeemer and Deliverer of captives; the holy war alludes to a vindictive deity of nationalism.

3. *Consistent with Christ.* The images and affections should be consistent with God's definitive revelation in Jesus Christ. For

Christians, the theological center of reference must be the saving event of Christ. Therefore, images from both Testaments must be gauged against the story of Jesus. He is the New Moses who leads God's people from slavery through his own Passover from death to life; the crusading warrior of the holy war is inconsistent with the character of Jesus presented in the New Testament.

4. *Fittingness.* The images and affections should be appropriate to the situation and shed light upon it. As Niebuhr argued, the image of God's healing judgment illumines the Allies' own responsibility for letting the world slide toward war. The image of retributive justice, of "setting the scales right," leads to self-deception and denial of any responsibility.

5. *Moral Rightness.* Finally, these images should indicate courses of action that concur with the standards of ordinary human morality. Christians may well be called to a way of life that is more demanding than ordinary morality, but they most assuredly are not called by God to behavior that is patently harmful to themselves or others. There is a public test on religious inspiration: it cannot violate the standards of human morality.[39]

Recall the various sources of Christian ethics: Scripture, tradition, moral philosophy and empirical data. Any coherent argument will draw on all these sources in an integrated way. Our selection of biblical material must be justified by the other sources we use: theological validity in the tradition, consistency with the normative portrait of the human person found in ethics, and relevance to the factual situation as determined by the best empirical analyses available. Niebuhr warns against "evil imaginations of the heart," symbols that send us down false ways and evoke self-centered affections. They obscure the truth of who we are and what we are doing. Evil imaginations of the heart are detected by the consequences they lead to, just as concepts are invalidated by their erroneous results.[40]

Test Case: The Maleness of Jesus and Contemporary Feminism

I have argued that the story of Jesus is normative for the identity of the Christian community and its members. This raises one of the most difficult issues for contemporary Christianity. Is maleness so central to the identity of Jesus that he cannot serve as the Christian prototype? Ironically, both post-Christian feminists and Vatican declarations on the ordination of women fall into the same trap: they make a peripheral aspect of Jesus central to the paradigm. They accept an iconic Jesus rather than one which can be understood analogically. Some rejectionist feminists flatly declare that a male figure cannot save women. More mainstream feminists argue that concentrating on the maleness of Jesus blinds one to his saving and liberating potential.[41] Jesus Christ is the prototype of liberation not because he is male but despite it. The multiple images from the story of Jesus are mutually corrective, restoring a paradigmatic rather than an iconic norm. Other theologians seem to suggest that contemporary Christians should shift from the concreteness of Jesus of Nazareth to more generic terms: the Christ, Spirit, Logos or Sophia. Schüssler Fiorenza points to an original community of disciples as the prototype of Christian equality and liberation.[42] Womanist theologians object to this move away from concreteness, as shown in Jacquelyn Grant's recent work *White Women's Christ and Black Women's Jesus*.[43]

Womanist theologians seem to concur with Latin American liberationists: Jesus of Nazareth is indispensable for Christian identity and action. Jon Sobrino has said that the figure of Jesus is more accessible to Latin American Christians than to middle class European or Americans. While more generic terms can bring out virtualities obscured by traditional Christologies, they can be problematic. If the argument in this chapter is correct, substituting abstractions for Jesus can leave Christian moral reflection imaginatively impoverished and affectively confused. Wisdom is a quality, not a story that can shape an identity. Equality and inclusiveness are important values but they do not make disciples; they cannot convey the full range of affective guidance offered in the gospels. For that we have to return to the concrete universal who is not the terminus of faith but who is the Way that has come to meet us.

Conclusion

Each of the five models of using Scripture has a distinctive contribution to make to Christian ethics; they make use of different portions of the Word of God and highlight different dimensions of the moral life. The model of responding love is not presented as the definitive approach but as a constructive account which spells out the implications of character and virtue ethics, which is emerging as an important way of doing ethics today. It also brings some more systematic attention to bear on the appeal to spirituality as the bridge between theory and action. Some of the liberation theologians who have the richest spirituality unfortunately have a relatively thin account of ethics. And some of those with the most developed systematic ethics, the natural law thinkers, have the least developed spirituality. When the resources of character and virtue ethics are brought to bear on biblical material, it can yield a more ethically sophisticated account of Christian experience than spirituality can offer by itself. Virtue ethics can raise the imaginative and affective dimensions of moral experience to critical reflection to show how rich the moral life is and how pervasive the guidance of Scripture can be in the mature Christian and the authentic Christian community.

In the introduction, I remarked that hermeneutics tends to bring us to the edge of ethics but then draws back. The task of *interpreting* Scripture is complicated and morally challenging since it demands virtues of honesty, self-critical awareness, and sensitivity to contemporary issues. The task of *responding* to the One revealed in Scripture calls forth a more extensive range of virtues, from compassion to justice, to the forgiveness that enables one to remain part of an actual community of faith, to the courage to endure what inevitably comes to those who live as if the Reign of God were coming into their world.

The position we called "responsive love" concentrates on the moral agent more than on the moral act. Or better, it holds that the wise and loving action comes from an agent who is becoming wise and loving. From the gradual transformation of the agent's affections we can expect Christian conduct to flow "naturally." Yet this is not only an internal reorganization of the person's moral psychology. The goodness of the friend, the needs of the neighbor, the cry of the poor, the plight of God's creation, and the lives of those to whom we are especially committed, all evoke the dispositions which give shape to the Christian character. Ethics draws its demand from the near and far neighbor because that is where God's invitation to service and self-gift calls out. The love of

Christ impels us and the beauty of Christ draws us, which is the same as saying that the Reign of God is already and not yet here. Christian duty is grounded in beauty and need, gratitude and hope.

What role do moral rules play in this ethics of Christian agency? They are definitely not the source of moral conduct, because imperatives on their own cannot produce affections. The deep commitments of the heart are evoked by their objects, the needs and goodness of the neighbor and the qualities of God revealed in history. Virtuous affections can guide the moral agent to interpret rules and apply them with that sensitivity we call discernment. In sum, the following of Christ comes out of participation in God's love and in compassionate identification with the neighbor rather than by inference from norms, even though norms may be indispensable in guiding compassion to act wisely.

Most contemporary Christian ethics does not use the Bible as a sourcebook of moral norms. Most of the authors we investigated propose an illuminative rather than a prescriptive use of Scripture. Decisions should be made in light of the central concerns and commitments of the canonical text, but decisions are not directly derived from biblical prescriptions. The Christian draws direction and a basic orientation from biblical faith. Other sources of moral wisdom, including moral philosophy and appropriate empirical data, are needed to determine the proper course of action. The role of rules in morality received the least attention in the authors surveyed. In part, this was due to the theoretical nature of their projects: they were not primarily addressing specific moral problems. A more fundamental issue lies in translating biblical imperatives for the Church today.

Most theologians who employ the Bible today consider it to be the normative statement of Christian identity. Whatever additional moral insight we derive from ethics or the social sciences must be tested against the portrait of God and of Christ found in Scripture. Jesus did not, however, proclaim simply a moral message; rather, he announced an event, the breaking in of the reign of God. Most theologians would agree with James Gustafson that Scripture does not present a revealed morality but a revealed reality.[44] The theologian must find ways of describing that reality so that moral insight can be gained for responding to God's action.

The problem of cultural distance between our era and biblical times has stimulated theologians to seek the underlying concerns and commitments of the Word of God that still apply. They have turned to a wider range of literature in the canon to find elements that express these enduring challenges—to story and symbol, to prophetic rhetoric and apocalyptic, to parable and doctrinal exposition. New attention needs to be given to biblical imperatives because moral imperatives play an indispensable part in reflective living. We need to practice most forms of behavior in order to appreciate their value. Humane behavior is not only the expression of virtues; it is usually also their foundation. The merciful will obtain mercy because they know what it looks like; the arrogant and vengeful will be blind to the mercy that God offers them. In addition, the imperatives of the Gospel have a radical quality that forces us to consider the distance between our ordinary motives and the revolutionary novelty of the Reign of God. The prohibition on divorce, the admonition to turn the other cheek, the mandate to invite the homeless to our dinner parties call us to acknowledge the gap between our ways and God's ways. They have an eminently practical religious impact which can be diluted if they are rephrased in more abstract terms.

These practical mandates are radical because the gift of God in Christ is radical. They connect the Christian with the historical person of Jesus Christ and the specific way of life that remains a surprise and a scandal. David Tracy describes the effect on Christian moral reflection that this challenge of the historical Jesus produces:

> The memory of Jesus confronts all sentimentalized notions of love with the intensified extremity of the actual thing in the remembered life of Jesus of Nazareth: compassion and conflict; preference for the outcasts, the poor, the oppressed; love of the enemy; love as hard other-regard that looks to the strength of the kind of love present in Jesus' ministry, expressed in his cross, vindicated by God in his resurrection; love as a freedom for the other that comes as gift and command from the strength of God to disallow the resentful weakness of the too-familiar caricatures of that love as mere "niceness."[45]

As more attention is given to the practical imperatives of Scripture, the unique call contained in the particular gift of Jesus of Nazareth may better school our hearts and deeds. This call to a distinctive way of life, these scandalous requirements, reveal the depth of God's empowerment in the gift of his love. Foundational theological truths and the moral understanding of the agent provide the context to interpret these practical requirements, but to grasp the gift we finally have to hear and act upon the gracious call contained in the gift of God.

Notes

Introduction

1. Wolfgang Schrage, *The Ethics of the New Testament* (Philadelphia: Fortress: 1988); Willi Marxsen, *New Testament Foundations for Christian Ethics* (Minneapolis: Fortress, 1993); also Pheme Perkins, "Ethics: New Testament," in David Noel Freedman (ed.), *The Anchor Bible Dictionary* vol. 2 (New York: Doubleday, 1992), pp. 652–665. For OT ethics see Bruce C. Birch, *Let Justice Roll Down: The Old Testament, Ethics, and Christian Life* (Louisville: Westminster/John Knox Press, 1991).

2. David H. Kelsey has argued that the notions of Scripture, canon, and community are interdependent in *The Uses of Scripture in Recent Theology* (Philadelphia: Fortress, 1975).

3. John Howard Yoder, *The Politics of Jesus* (Grand Rapids: Wm. Eerdmans Publishing Co., 1972), p. 80. See John R. Donahue, S.J., "The Challenge of the Biblical Renewal to Moral Theology," in William J. O'Brien (ed.), *Riding Time Like a River: The Catholic Moral Tradition Since Vatican II* (Washington, D.C.: Georgetown University Press, 1993), pp. 59–80. Donahue discusses Pope Pius XII's encyclical *Divino Afflante Spiritu* and Vatican II's *Dogmatic Constitution on Divine Revelation (Dei Verbum)*.

4. See David Tracy, *The Analogical Imagination* (New York: Crossroad, 1981).

5. See Raymond E. Brown, S.S. and Sandra M. Schneiders. I.H.M, "Hermeneutics," in Raymond E. Brown, S.S., Joseph A. Fitzmyer, S.J., and Roland E. Murphy, O.Carm. (eds.), *The New Jerome Biblical*

Commentary (Englewood Cliffs, New Jersey: Prentice-Hall, 1990), pp. 1146–1165.

6. Thomas W. Ogletree, *The Use of the Bible in Christian Ethics: A Constructive Essay* (Philadelphia: Fortress, 1983), pp. 15–45.

7. Ogletree, *Use of the Bible*, p. 4.

8. J.I.H. McDonald, *Biblical Interpretation and Christian Ethics* (Cambridge: Cambridge University Press, 1993), p. 244.

9. Sandra M. Schneiders, *The Revelatory Text: Interpreting the New Testament as Sacred Scripture* (San Francisco: HarperCollins, 1991) p. 168.

10. Ibid., p. 171.

11. Ibid., p. 173.

12. Lisa Sowle Cahill, "The New Testament and Ethics: Communities of Social Change," *Interpretation* (December 1990), p. 40, referring to Wayne Meeks, *The Moral World of the First Christians* (Philadelphia: Westminster, 1986).

13. Cahill, ibid., p. 43. For an excellent investigation of how the New Testament's teaching on violence was interpreted by different eras, see Cahill's *Love Your Enemies: Discipleship, Pacifism, and Just War Theory* (Philadelphia: Fortress, 1994).

14. Walter Brueggemann, *The Prophetic Imagination,* (Philadelphia: Fortress Press, 1978), and *Interpretation and Obedience: From Faithful Reading to Faithful Living* (Minneapolis: Fortress, 1991).

15. *The Five Gospels: The Search for the Authentic Words of Jesus* (New York: Macmillan, 1994).

16. Paul Ricoeur, "Toward a Hermeneutic of the Idea of Revelation," *Harvard Theological Review* (January–April 1971), pp. 1–19. See also David L. Bartlett, *The Shape of Biblical Authority* (Philadelphia: Fortress, 1983).

17. Richard B. Hays, "Scripture-Shaped Community: The Problem of Method in New Testament Ethics," *Interpretation* (July 1990), p. 46.

18. Richard N. Longenecker, *New Testament Social Ethics for Today* (Grand Rapids: William B. Eerdmans Publishing Co., 1984), p. 92.

19. Ogletree, *Use of Bible*, p. 11.

20. See ibid., p. 199. See also Ogletree, *Hospitality to the Stranger: Dimensions of Moral Understanding* (Philadelphia: Fortress, 1985), pp. 135–145.

21. Ogletree, *Use of the Bible*, p. 202.

22. National Conference of Catholic Bishops, *The Challenge of Peace* (Washington, D.C.: United States Catholic Conference, 1983) and *Economic Justice for All* (Washington, D.C.: U.S.C.C., 1986).

23. N.C.C.B., *Economic Justice for All*, par. 79.

24. Gene Outka, *Agape: An Ethical Analysis* (New Haven: Yale University Press, 1972).

25. Richard Hays, "Scripture-Shaped Community," p. 50.

1. The Command of God

1. Dietrich Bonhoeffer, *The Cost of Discipleship* (New York: Macmillan Publishing Co., 1963).

2. Ibid., p. 99.

3. Martin Luther, "The Freedom of a Christian," in *Martin Luther. Selections from His Writings*, ed. by John Dillenberger (Garden City, New York: Doubleday and Co., 1961), p, 76.

4. Bonhoeffer, *Discipleship*, p. 47.

5. Ibid., p. 63.

6. Ibid., p. 88.

7. Ibid., p. 69.

8. James M. Gustafson, *Christ and the Moral Life* (New York: Harper and Row Publishers, 1968).

9. Bonhoeffer, *Discipleship*, p. 96.

10. D. Bonhoeffer, *Ethics*, edited by Eberhard Bethge (New York: The Macmillan Co., 1955), pp. 50–51.

11. Bonhoeffer, *Discipleship*, p. 250.

12. Bonhoeffer, *Ethics*, pp. 277–302.

13. Karl Barth, *Epistle to the Romans* (London: Oxford University Press, 1960).

14. See Krister Stendahl, "The Apostle Paul and the Introspective Conscience of the West," in *Paul Among Jews and Gentiles and Other Essays* (Philadelphia: Westminster Press, 1976).

15. See Timothy P. Weber, "The Two-Edged Sword: The Fundamentalist Use of the Bible," in Nathan O. Hatch and Mark A. Noll (eds.), *The Bible in America* (New York: Oxford University Press, 1982), pp. 101–120.

16. Karl Barth, *Church Dogmatics* II/2, ed. by G.W. Bromiley and T.F. Torrance (Edinburgh: T. and T. Clark, 1957), p. 609.

17. Ibid., p. 618.

18. Ibid., p. 682.

19. Ibid., p. 697.

20. Ibid., p. 557.

21. Ibid., p. 584.

22. Ibid., p. 585.

23. Ibid., p. 574.

24. Karl Barth, *Church Dogmatics* IV/2, ed. by G.W. Bromiley and T.F. Torrance (Edinburgh: T. and T. Clark, 1958), pp. 533–613.

25. Karl Barth, *Church Dogmatics* III/4, ed. by G.W. Bromiley and T.F. Torrance (Edinburgh: T. and T. Clark, 1961), pp. 324–470.

26. Ibid., p. 407.

27. Ibid., p. 412.

28. Ibid., p. 421.

29. Ibid., p. 430.

30. Ibid., p. 449.

31. Richard J. Mouw, *The God Who Commands* (Notre Dame, Ind.; University of Notre Dame Press, 1990), p. 19. See also Mouw, "The Bible in Twentieth Century Protestantism: A Preliminary Taxonomy," in Hatch and Noll (eds.), *The Bible in America*, pp. 139–162.

32. Ibid., p. 186.

33. Donald G. Bloesch, *Freedom for Obedience: Evangelical Ethics for Contemporary Times* (San Francisco: Harper & Row, Publishers, 1987), p. 140.

34. Ibid., pp. 216–217.

2. Scripture as Moral Reminder

1. Fuchs suggested to the author that this chapter be entitled "Scripture as Moral Reminder" rather than "Moral Teacher" since the latter would imply that humanity is ignorant of its moral responsibilities without the teaching of revelation.

2. Pope John Paul II, *Veritatis Splendor: Encyclical Letter Addressed to All the Bishops of the Catholic Church Regarding Certain*

Fundamental Questions of the Church's Moral Teaching (Vatican City: Libreria Editrice Vaticana, 1993).

3. See Bruno Schüller, S.J., "A Contribution to the Theological Discussion of Natural Law," in Charles E. Curran and Richard A. McCormick, S.J., eds., *Readings in Moral Theology, No. 7: Natural Law and Theology* (New York: Paulist Press, 1991), p. 77.

4. Schüller, ibid., p. 79.

5. John Macquarrie, *Three Issues in Ethics* (New York: Harper and Row, Publishers, 1970), p. 91.

6. Josef Fuchs, S.J., *Natural Law: A Theological Investigation* (New York: Sheed and Ward, 1965).

7. Thomas Aquinas, *Summa Theologiae* I–IIae, Ques. 106, art. 1.

8. Josef Fuchs, S.J., *Moral Demands & Personal Obligations* (Washington, D.C.: Georgetown University Press, 1993), p. 218.

9. Josef Fuchs, *Christian Morality: The Word Becomes Flesh* (Washington, D.C.: Georgetown University Press, 1987), p. 13.

10. Ibid., pp. 87, 88.

11. Ibid., p. 92. See Bruno Schüller, S.J., "The Debate on the Specific Character of a Christian Ethics: Some Remarks," in *Readings in Moral Theology No. 2* ed. by Curran and McCormick.

12. Schüller, "Theological Discussion of Natural Law," p. 89.

13. Thomas Aquinas, *Summa Theologiae* I–IIae.

14. Josef Fuchs, S.J., "Is There a Specifically Christian Morality?" in *Readings in Moral Theology No. 2* ed. by Charles E. Curran and Richard A. McCormick, S.J. (New York: Paulist Press, 1980), p 12.

15. Vincent MacNamara, *Faith and Ethics: Recent Roman Catholicism* (Washington, D.C.: Georgetown University Press, 1985), p. 100.

16. Ibid., p. 106.

17. Ibid., p. 108.

18. Ibid., p. 171.

19. James Gaffney, *Matters of Faith and Morals* (Kansas City, Mo.: Sheed and Ward, 1987), p. 146.

20. Schüller, "Theological Discussion of Natural Law," p. 83.

21. See John Wilkins, ed., *Considering Veritatis Splendor* (Cleveland: Pilgrim Press, 1994) which includes the text of the encyclical.

22. The bishops at Vatican II cautioned that the magisterium cannot be expected to have all the answers; unfortunately, this point is not mentioned in "The Splendor of Truth." "Let the layman not imagine

that his pastors are always such experts that to every problem which arises, however complicated, they can readily give him a concrete solution, or even that such is their mission. Rather, enlightened by Christian wisdom and giving close attention to the teaching authority of the Church, let the layman take on his own distinctive role." Second Vatican Council, *Gaudium et Spes, Documents of Vatican II*, ed. Walter Abbott, S.J. (New York: America Press, 1966), p. 244.

23. John Mahoney, *The Making of Moral Theology: A Study of the Roman Catholic Tradition* (Oxford: Clarendon Press, 1987), p. 174.

3. Call to Liberation

1. For a collection of representative of various liberation theologies see Susan Brooks Thistlewaite and Mary Potter Engel (eds.), *Lift Every Voice: Constructing Christian Theologies from the Underside* (San Francisco: Harper & Row, 1990).

2. See Emilie M. Townes (ed.), *A Troubling in My Soul: Womanist Perspectives on Evil & Suffering* (Maryknoll: Orbis Books, 1993).

3. See Gustavo Gutierrez, "Option for the Poor," in Ignacio Ellacuria, S.J. and Jon Sobrino, S.J., eds., *Mysterium Liberationis: Fundamental Concepts of Liberation Theology* (Maryknoll: Orbis Books, 1993), pp. 236–238; also, Elisabeth Schüssler Fiorenza, *But She Said: Feminist Practices of Biblical Interpretation* (Boston: Beacon Press, 1992), pp. 150–156.

4. Cited in Jon Sobrino, "Spirituality and the Following of Jesus," in Ignacio Ellacuria, S.J. and Jon Sobrino, S.J., eds. *Mysterium Liberationis: Fundamental Concepts of Liberation Theology* (Maryknoll: Orbis Books, 1993), p. 693.

5. Ibid., p. 687.

6. Gustavo Gutierrez, *A Theology of Liberation* (Maryknoll, N.Y.: Orbis Books, 1988), is the second edition, revised with a new introduction by the author of the original version that was published in 1971 and appeared in English from Orbis Books in 1973. All quotations and citations here will be from the 1988 edition. For the best North American evaluation of liberation theology see Arthur F. McGovern, *Liberation Theology and Its Critics: Toward an Assessment* (Maryknoll: Orbis Books, 1989).

7. Gustavo Gutierrez, *The Power of the Poor in History: Selected Writings* (Maryknoll: Orbis Books, 1983), p. 208.

8. Gustavo Gutierrez, "Option for the Poor," in *Mysterium Liberationis*, p. 240.

9. Sobrino, *Mysterium Liberationis*, p. 691.

10. Gutierrez, *Power of the Poor*, pp. 71–72.

11. See Gustavo Gutierrez, *The God of Life* (Maryknoll: Orbis Books, 1991), esp. pp. 15–19. For the most succinct account of the biblical foundations of liberation theology, see "God's Revelation and Proclamation in History," in *Power of the Poor*, pp. 3–22.

12. Gutierrez, *God of Life*, p. 162.

13. Gustavo Gutierrez, *On Job: God-Talk and the Suffering of the Innocent* (Maryknoll: Orbis Books, 1987), pp. 93–103. See the insightful discussion of Thomas L. Schubeck, S.J., *Liberation Ethics: Sources, Models, and Norms* (Minneapolis: Fortress Press, 1993), pp. 161–168.

14. Gutierrez, *God of Life*, p. 118.

15. Ibid., pp. 132–133.

16. Gustavo Gutierrez, *We Drink From Our Own Wells: The Spiritual Journey of a People* (Maryknoll: Orbis Books, 1984).

17. See Norman K. Gottwald, *The Tribes of Yahweh: A Sociology of Liberated Israel* (Maryknoll: Orbis Books, 1979). For another materialist reading of the Old Testament, see Jose Miranda, *Marx and the Bible* (Maryknoll: Orbis Books, 1974).

18. Gilberto da Silva Gorgulho, "Biblical Hermeneutics," in *Mysterium Liberationis*, p. 134. Against a materialist interpretation, see Norbert F. Lohfink, S.J., who argues that a strictly horizontal reading of Exodus misses the surprising element, the active role of Yahweh, which is uniquely present in this experience of Israel in contrast to its neighbors: Lohfink, *Option for the Poor: The Basic Principle of Liberation Theology in the Light of the Bible* (Berkeley, Ca.: BIBAL Press, 1987).

19. A different theology could interpret the exodus in a way that draws opposite moral conclusions about revolutionary violence. John Howard Yoder makes just such an argument in support for his Mennonite pacifism in *The Politics of Jesus* (Grand Rapids: Wm. Eerdmans Publishing Co., 1972).

20. Walter Rauschenbusch, *Christianizing the Social Order* (New York: Macmillan, 1912).

21. Gutierrez, *Theology of Liberation*, p. 103.

22. Ibid.

23. Jon Sobrino, *Jesus the Liberator: A Historical-Theological Reading of Jesus of Nazareth* (Maryknoll: Orbis Books, 1993), p. 61.

24. Ibid., p. 196.

25. Jon Sobrino, "Central Position of the Reign of God in Liberation Theology," in *Mysterium Liberationis*, p. 366.

26. Ibid., p. 354.

27. Sobrino, *Jesus the Liberator*, p. 210.

28. Sobrino, *Mysterium Liberationis*, p. 363.

29. Ibid., p. 370.

30. See ibid., p. 370.

31. See MacNamara, *Faith and Ethics*, pp. 136–141.

32. Jose Miguez Bonino, *Toward a Christian Political Ethics* (Philadelphia: Fortress Press, 1983), p. 107, cited in Schubeck's analysis of Miguez Bonino's ethics in *Liberation Ethics*, p. 221.

33. Enrique Dussel, *Ethics and Community* (Maryknoll: Orbis Books, 1988).

34. Sobrino, *Mysterium Liberationis*, p. 380.

35. Jon Sobrino, *Spirituality of Liberation: Toward Political Holiness* (Maryknoll: Orbis Books, 1988), p. 2.

36. Sobrino, "Spirituality and the Following of Jesus," in *Mysterium Liberationis*, p. 687.

37. Schubeck, *Liberation Ethics*, p. 168.

38. Sobrino, *Mysterium Liberationis*, p. 698.

39. Mary Ann Tolbert, "Defining the Problem: The Bible and Feminist Hermeneutics," *semeia* 28 (1983), pp. 122–123. Rosemary Radford Ruether exemplifies the first type and Phyllis L. Trible the second, according to Tolbert.

40. Elisabeth Schüssler Fiorenza, *In Memory of Her: A Feminist Theological Reconstruction of Christian Origins* (New York: Crossroad, 1984).

41. Schüssler Fiorenza, *But She Said*, p. 32.

42. Ibid., p. 96.

43. See Paul Ricoeur, *Freud and Philosophy: An Essay on Interpretations* (New Haven: Yale University Press, 1970).

44. Schüssler Fiorenza, *But She Said*, p. 12.

45. Elisabeth Schüssler Fiorenza, *Bread Not Stone: The Challenge of Feminist Biblical Interpretation* (Boston: Beacon Press, 1984), p. 60. A similar criticism was made of Sobrino's appeal to the historical Jesus on historical critical grounds by John P. Meier in "The Bible as Source for Theology," in *Proceedings of the Catholic Theological Society of America* 43 (1988), pp. 3–4.

46. Schüssler Fiorenza, *But She Said*, p. 36.

47. Schüssler Fiorenza, *Bread Not Stone*, p. xxiii.

48. Schüssler Fiorenza, *But She Said*, p. 149. Cf. *Bread Not Stone*, pp. 14, 61, 88.

49. Schüssler Fiorenza, *But She Said*, p. 76.

50. Ibid., p. 157.

51. Ibid., p. 158.

52. "Such a writing of G-d is meant to indicate that G-d is "in a religious sense unnameable" and belongs to the 'realm of the ineffable.' G-d is not G-d's 'proper name.'" *But She Said*, p. 220. See Rebecca S. Chopp, *The Power to Speak: Feminism, Language, God* (New York: Crossroad, 1989), 32.

53. Tolbert, "Defining the Problem," p. 124. Raymond E. Brown criticizes Schüssler Fiorenza on the same score: "If the surface biblical narrative does not offer enough material to support such a feminist cause, maximum usage of the slightest clues is thought to lead to detecting more favorable situations that have been suppressed consciously or unconsciously. To others these advocacy reconstructions seem forced...one must deal with the possibility that the biblical authors were unconscious of or uninterested in issues that seem important to us." See Raymond E. Brown, S.S. and Sandra M. Schneiders, I.H.M., "Hermeneutics," in Raymond E. Brown, S.S., Joseph A. Fitzmyer, S.J., and Roland E. Murphy, O. Carm,. eds. *The New Jerome Biblical Commentary* (Englewood Cliffs, New Jersey: Prentice-Hall, Inc., 1990), p. 1162.

54. Sobrino, Spirituality of Liberation, pp. 27–29; *Mysterium Liberationis*, p. 691.

55. Anthony C. Thiselton, *New Horizons in Hermeneutics: The Theory and Practice of Transforming Biblical Reading* (Grand Rapids: Zondervan/HarperCollins, 1992), pp. 451–452.

56. See the interviews with Brazilian women activists and pastors in

Mev Puleo, *The Struggle is One: Voices and Visions of Liberation* (Albany: State University of New York Press, 1994).

57. Lisa Sowle Cahill, *Between the Sexes: Foundations for a Christian Ethics of Sexuality* (Philadelphia: Fortress Press, 1985), chapter three. See Phyllis Trible, *God and the Rhetoric of Sexuality* (Philadelphia: Fortress Press, 1978)

58. Sandra M. Schneiders, "The Bible and Feminism," in Catherine Mowry La Cugna, ed., *Freeing Theology: The Essentials of Theology in Feminist Perspective* (San Francisco: HarperCollins, 1993), pp. 48–49. See Schneiders' important work on hermeneutics, *The Revelatory Text: Interpreting the New Testament as Sacred Scripture* (San Francisco: HarperCollins, 1991).

4. Call to Discipleship

1. John R. Donahue, S.J., *The Gospel in Parable: Metaphor, Narrative, and Theology in the Synoptic Gospels* (Philadelphia: Fortress Press, 1988).

2. Stanley Hauerwas, *Character and the Christian Life* (San Antonio: Trinity University Press, 1975); *Vision and Virtue: Essays in Christian Ethical Reflection* (Notre Dame: Fides/Claretian Publishers, 1974); *Truthfulness and Tragedy: Further Investigations into Christian Ethics* (Notre Dame: University of Notre Dame Press, 1977); *A Community of Character: Toward a Constructive Christian Social Ethic* (Notre Dame: University of Notre Dame Press, 1981).

3. Stanley Hauerwas, *The Peaceable Kingdom: A Primer in Christian Ethics* (Notre Dame: University of Notre Dame Press, 1983); *Suffering Presence: Theological Reflections on Medicine, the Mentally Handicapped, and the Church* (Notre Dame: University of Notre Dame Press, 1986); *Against the Nations: War and Survival in A Liberal Society* (Notre Dame: University of Notre Dame Press, 1992); *Unleashing the Scripture: Freeing the Bible from Captivity to America* (Nashville: Abingdon, 1993).

4. Hauerwas, *A Community of Character*, p. 48.

5. Hauerwas, *Against the Nations*, p. 56.

6. Hauerwas, *Unleashing the Scripture*, pp. 66, 67.

7. Ibid., p. 69

8. Hauerwas, *Peaceable Kingdom*, p. 85.

9. See Alasdair MacIntyre, *After Virtue: A Study in Moral Theory* (Notre Dame: University of Notre Dame Press, 1981), especially chapters four through six.

10. Hauerwas acknowledges the formative influence which H. Richard Niebuhr's *The Meaning of Revelation* had on him: Niebuhr, *The Meaning of Revelation* (New York: The Macmillan Co., 1960); see Hauerwas, *Unleashing the Scripture*, pp. 84–86.

11. Hauerwas, *Unleashing the Scripture*, pp. 25–26.

12. Hauerwas, *Against the Nations*, p. 58.

13. Ibid., p. 112.

14. Stephen E. Fowl and L. Gregory Jones, *Reading in Communion: Scripture and Ethics in Christian Life* (Grand Rapids, William B. Eerdmans Publishing Co., 1991), p. 31.

15. Hauerwas, *Suffering Presence*, p. 31.

16. Ibid., p. 79.

17. Hauerwas, *Against the Nations*, p. 117.

18. Ibid., p. 128.

19. Ibid., p. 197; see also p. 128.

20. Fowl and Jones, *Reading in Communion*, p. 10.

21. Hauerwas, *Against the Nations*, p. 115. For more extended discussion on natural law, see *The Peaceable Kingdom*, chapter four.

22. Ibid., p. 44.

23. Hauerwas, *Truthfulness and Tragedy*, p. 35.

24. Paul Lauritzen, "Is 'Narrative' Really a Panacea? The Use of 'Narrative' in the Work of Metz and Hauerwas," *The Journal of Religion* 67 no. 3 (1987), p. 336. See also Jeffrey Stout, *Flight from Authority* (Notre Dame: University of Notre Dame, 1981).

25. Ibid., p. 338; see also William Schweiker, "Iconoclasts, Builders, and Dramatists: The Use of Scripture in Theological Ethics," *The Annual of the Society of Christian Ethics* (1986), pp. 129–162.

26. Stanley M. Hauerwas, *Christian Existence Today: Essays on Church, World and Living in Between* (Durham, N.C.: Labyrinth Press, 1988), pp. 9, 10; see James Gustafson, "The Sectarian Temptation: Reflections on Theology, the Church, and the University" *Proceedings of the Catholic Theological Society of America* 40 (1985), pp. 83–94.

27. Paul Nelson, *Narrative and Morality: A Theological Inquiry* (University Park, Pa: Pennsylvania State Press, 1989), p. 149; see also

Garrett Green, ed., *Scriptural Authority and Narrative Interpretation* (Philadelphia: Fortress Press, 1987), especially chapters by Maurice Wiles, Stephen Crites, David H. Kelsey, Gene Outka, and George Lindbeck.

28. Ibid., p. 149.

29. Nelson, *Narrative* 83–84. Anyone doubting Nelson's caveats should read Michael Goldberg's spirited disagreement with Ronald Thiemann's interpretation of Israel's narrative in "God, Action and Narrative: *Which* Narrative? *Which* Action? *Which* God?" *Journal of Religion* 68 no. 1 (1988), pp. 39–56. See also Goldberg, *Jews and Christians, Getting our Stories Straight: The Exodus and the Passion-Resurrection* (Nashville: Abingdon, 1985).

30. William Wimsatt, *The Verbal Icon: Studies in the Meaning of Poetry* (Lexington, Ky.: University of Kentucky Press, 1954), p. 71. Cited in John A. Donahue, S.J., *The Gospel in Parable: Metaphor, Narrative, and Theology in the Synoptic Gospels* (Philadelphia: Fortress Press, 1988), p. 14. The latter book includes a comprehensive bibliography of the abundant material on parable that has appeared in the last two decades. See also Pheme Perkins, *Hearing the Parables of Jesus* (New York: Paulist, 1981).

31. C.H. Dodd, *The Parables of the Kingdom* (New York: Charles Scribner's Sons, 1961), p. 5.

32. Donahue, *Gospel in Parable*, p. 19.

33. Ibid., p. 17; see also p. 151.

34. James M. Gustafson, "The Place of Scripture in Ethics: A Methodological Study," in *Theology and Christian Ethics* (Philadelphia: Pilgrim Press, 1974), p. 121.

35. George W. Stroup, *The Promise of Narrative Theology: Recovering the Gospel in the Church* (Atlanta: John Knox Press, 1981), pp. 144, 209.

36. Donahue, *Gospel in Parable*, p. 132. See Benedict M. Guevin, "The Moral Imagination and the Shaping Power of the Parables," *Journal of Religious Ethics* 17 (1989), pp. 63–79.

37. Ibid., p. 198. See also Robert A. Krieg, C.S.C., *Story-Shaped Christology: The Role of Narratives in Identifying Jesus Christ* (New York: Paulist, 1988), which shows the connection between Gospel and the response of faith by interweaving his theology with the narrative of Dorothy Day's life.

38. Ibid., p. 11.

39. Sallie McFague, *Metaphorical Theology: Models of God in Religious Language* (Philadelphia: Fortress, 1983), p. 39; see also her *Speaking in Parables: A Study in Metaphor and Theology* (Philadelphia: Fortress, 1975).

40. McFague, *Metaphorical Theology*, p. 46.

41. Robert W. Funk, *Language, Hermeneutic and the Word of God: The Problem of Language in the New Testament and Contemporary Theology* (New York: Harper & Row, 1966), pp. 193–196.

5. Scripture as Basis for Responding Love

1. John P. Meier, "The Historical Jesus: Rethinking Some Concepts," *Theological Studies* 51/1 (1990), p. 22.

2. See Jon Sobrino, *Spirituality of Liberation: Toward Political Holiness* (Maryknoll, N.Y.: Orbis, 1988), p. 130.

3. William Wimsatt, *The Verbal Icon: Studies in the Meaning of Poetry* (Lexington, Ky.: University of Kentucky Press, 1954), p. 71.

4. Sandra M. Schneiders points out the dangers of selective use of the canon of Scripture, even of rejecting oppressive biblical texts. See her "The Bible and Feminism: Biblical Theology," in Catherine Mowrey LaCugna, *Freeing Theology: The Essentials of Theology in Feminist Perspective* (San Francisco: HarperCollins, 1993), pp. 31–57. My approach is indebted to her *The Revelatory Text: Interpreting the New Testament as Sacred Scripture* (San Francisco: HarperCollins, 1991).

5. For examples: Jesus Christ is the symbolic form used to interpret experience (H. Richard Niebuhr); the qualities expressed in God's dealings with humans ought to shape and inform the dispositions of believers (James Gustafson); the moral response must conform to the shape of the engendering deed (Joseph Sittler); the gospel narrative should render a community of character that embodies its concerns (Stanley Hauerwas); and the dangerous and repressed memories of Jesus evoke corresponding hopes and actions in the community of disciples (J.B. Metz, David Tracy, Elisabeth Schüssler Fiorenza).

6. Some authors prefer to characterize moral reflection as metaphorical rather than analogical to emphasize its patterned and

figured nature: see Mark Johnson, *Moral Imagination: Implications of Cognitive Science for Ethics* (Chicago: University of Chicago, 1993), pp. 53–61.

7. Elisabeth Schüssler Fiorenza, *Bread Not Stone: The Challenge of Feminist Biblical Interpretation* (Boston: Beacon Press, 1984), p. 14.

8. Garrett Green, *Imagining God: Theology and the Religious Imagination* (San Francisco: Harper & Row, 1989), p. 67: "Something serves as a paradigm by exhibiting a pattern, a coherent nexus of relations, in a simple and obvious way. Paradigms have a heuristic function, serving to reveal the larger patterns in broader areas of experience that might otherwise remain inaccessible because they appear incoherent or bewildering in their complexity." Ibid.

9. Michael Walzer, *Exodus and Revolution* (New York: Basic Books, 1985), p. 149. The quotation is from W. D. Davies, The *Territorial Dimension of Judaism* (Berkeley: University of California Press, 1982), p. 60.

10. Walzer, *Exodus and Revolution*, p. 134.

11. Albert R. Jonsen and Stephen Toulmin, *The Abuse of Casuistry: A History of Moral Reasoning* (Berkeley: University of California Press, 1988), p. 41.

12. Green, *Imagining God*, p. 72.

13. Ibid., p. 107

14. Gustafson, *Can Ethics Be Christian?* p. 115.

15. See Niebuhr, *Meaning of Revelation*, pp. 107–110.

16. H. Richard Niebuhr, *Meaning of Revelation*, p. 70.

17. Ibid., p. 72.

18. H. Richard Niebuhr, "War as the Judgment of God," *Christian Century* 59 (1942), pp. 630–33; "Is God in the War?" ibid., pp. 953–955; "War as Crucifixion," ibid. 60 (1943), pp. 513–515.

19. Niebuhr, "Judgment of God," p. 631.

20. Oscar Wilde, *De Profundis*, 1897, in H. Montgomery Hyde, ed., *The Annotated Oscar Wilde* (London: Orbis, 1982), cited in Ronald de Sousa, *The Rationality of Emotion* (Cambridge, Mass.: M.I.T. Press, 1990), p. 320.

21. For a discussion of controls on the use of imagination and appeal to affections, see below pp. 120–121; also, William C. Spohn, "The Reasoning Heart: An American Approach to Christian Discernment," *Theological Studies* 44/1 (1983), p. 43.

22. In the second chapter we noted that denying the wall of separation between motive and content means affirming that why and how we act enters into the moral meaning of what we do. Vincent MacNamara has made the case for the connection of motive and content in *Faith and Ethics: Recent Roman Catholicism* (Washington, D.C.: Georgetown University Press, 1985), pp. 103–110.

23. R. de Souza, *Rationality of Emotion*, p. 323.

24. James M. Gustafson, *Can Ethics Be Christian?* (Chicago: University of Chicago Press, 1975), p. 92.

25. Ibid., p. 101.

26. Jon Sobrino, *Jesus the Liberator: A Historical Theological View* (Maryknoll, N.Y.: Orbis, 1993), p. 171.

27. Sobrino, *Spirituality of Liberation*, p. 40.

28. H. Richard Niebuhr, *The Responsible Self: An Essay in Christian Moral Philosophy* (New York: Harper & Row, 1963), p. 155.

29. See Paul Ricouer, *The Symbolism of Evil* (Boston: Beacon Press, 1967), pp. 19–24.

30. Don E. Saliers, *The Soul in Paraphrase* (New York: Seabury Press, 1980), p. 13.

31. See Mark Johnson, *Moral Imagination: Implications of Cognitive Science for Ethics* (Chicago: University of Chicago Press, 1993), pp. 150–184. See also Mark Johnson and George Lakoff, *Metaphors We Live By* (Chicago: University of Chicago Press, 1980).

32. Mark Johnson, *Moral Imagination*, p. 170.

33. See Stephen E. Fowl and L. Gregory Jones, *Reading in Communion: Scripture and Ethics in Christian Life* (Grand Rapids: Eerdmans, 1991), 29–44. Also Lisa Sowle Cahill, "The New Testament and Ethics: Communities of Social Change, *Interpretation* 44 (1990), and Richard B. Hays, "Scripture-Shaped Community: The Problem of Method on New Testament Ethics," ibid., 42–55.

34. Jerome Murphy-O'Connor, O.P., *Becoming Human Together* (Wilmington, Del.: Michael Glazier, Inc., 1982), p. 214.

35. See Jonsen and Toulmin, *Abuse of Casuistry*, p. 318.

36. Phyllis Trible, *God and the Rhetoric of Sexuality* (Philadelphia: Fortress, 1978).

37. Anne E. Carr cites "a pluralism of images of Christ that are mutually corrective when viewed in connection with women's experience," in *Transforming Grace: Christian Tradition and Women's*

Experience (San Francisco: Harper & Row, 1988), 168. See also Harriet Crabtree, *The Christian Life: Traditional Metaphors and Contemporary Theologies.* Harvard Dissertations in Religion Series no. 29 (Minneapolis: Fortress, 1991); Elizabeth A. Johnson, *She Who Is: The Mystery of God in Feminist Theological Discourse* (New York: Crossroad, 1992), pp. 150–169.

38. Walzer, *Exodus and Revolution*, p. 139.

39. This set of criteria is indebted to James M. Gustafson: see his *Can Ethics Be Christian?* pp. 130–143.

40. Niebuhr, *Meaning of Revelation*, p. 73.

41. Rosemary Radford Ruether asks whether a male savior can help women in her *To Change the World: Christology and Cultural Criticism* (New York: Crossroad, 1981), pp. 45–56. See Elizabeth A. Johnson, "Redeeming the Name of Christ," in Catherine Mowry LaCugna, ed., *Freeing Theology*, pp. 115–137.

42. Elisabeth Schüssler Fiorenza, *In Memory of Her: A Feminist Theological Reconstruction of Christian Origins* (New York: Crossroad, 1983) and *Bread Not Stone: The Challenge of Feminist Biblical Interpretation* (Boston: Beacon Press, 1984).

43. Jacquelyn Grant, *White Women's Christ and Black Women's Jesus: Feminist Christology and Womanist Response* (Atlanta: Scholars Press, 1989).

44. James M. Gustafson, "The Place of Scripture in Ethics: A Methodological Study," in *Theology and Christian Ethics* (Philadelphia: Pilgrim Press, 1974), p. 121.

45. David Tracy, *The Analogical Imagination* (New York: Crossroad, 1981), p. 330.

Other Books in This Series

What are they saying about Christian-Jewish Relations?
by John T. Pawlikowski
What are they saying about Creation?
by Zachary Hayes, O.F.M.
What are they saying about the Prophets?
by David P. Reid, SS. CC.
What are they saying about Moral Norms?
by Richard M. Gula, S.S.
What are they saying about Sexual Morality?
by James P. Hanigan
What are they saying about Dogma?
by William E. Reiser, S.J.
What are they saying about Peace and War?
by Thomas A. Shannon
What are they saying about Papal Primacy?
by J. Michael Miller, C.S.B.
What are they saying about Matthew's Sermon on the Mount?
by Donald Senior, C.P.
What are they saying about Biblical Archaeology?
by Leslie J. Hoppe, O.F.M.
What are they saying about Theological Method?
by J.J. Mueller, S.J.
What are they saying about Virtue?
by Anthony J. Tambasco
What are they saying about Genetic Engineering?
by Thomas A. Shannon
What are they saying about Paul?
by Joseph Plevnik, S.J.
What are they saying about Salvation?
by Rev. Denis Edwards
What are they saying about Mark?
by Frank J. Matera
What are they saying about Luke?
by Mark Allan Powell
What are they saying about John?
by Gerard S. Sloyan
What are they saying about Acts?
by Mark Allan Powell

What are they saying about the Ministerial Priesthood?
by Rev. Daniel Donovan
What are they saying about the Social Setting of the New Testament?
by Carolyn Osiek
What are they saying about Unbelief?
by Michael Paul Gallagher, S.J.